What are human beings that you are mindful of them,
mortals that you care for them?

Yet you have made them a little lower than God,
and crowned them with glory and honor.

O Lord, our Sovereign, how majestic is your name in all the earth!

(NRSV Ps. 8:4, 5, 9)

In Praise of Virtue

An Exploration of the Biblical Virtues in a Christian Context

Benjamin W. Farley

William B. Eerdmans Publishing Company
Grand Rapids, Michigan

00 99 98 97 96 95   7 6 5 4 3 2 1

Library of Congress Cataloging-in-Publication Data

Farley, Benjamin Wirt.
    In praise of virtue: an exploration of the biblical virtues in a Christian
context / Benjamin W. Farley.
        p.   cm.
    Includes bibliographical references (p.   ).
    ISBN 0-8028-0792-5 (pbk.: alk. paper)
    1. Virtues — Biblical teaching. 2. Virtues. 3. Christian ethics — Reformed
(Reformed Church) authors. I. Title.
    BS680.V56F37 1995
    241'.4 — dc20   95-19179
                                                              CIP

to my sons
John and Bryan
and to
Gerald Calvin Lord

Contents

Preface

THE PRIMARY PURPOSE of this book is to identify, explore, and reflect on the virtues of the Old and the New Testaments and their relevance to the Christian life today. This book is intended for several audiences. First, it is written for the seminary student, whose courses in ethics and biblical studies seldom afford time for exploring the biblical virtues per se, let alone time for identifying them or investigating their significance for the Christian life. Second, it is written for Christian feminists in response to issues they have raised concerning humankind's creation in "the image of God" and the "revaluation of values" which the feminist critique invites. For some time, the feminists have argued that the "feminine experience" is sufficiently different from the masculine to require a fresh approach to woman herself and the kinds of values, goals, and nuances of self-expression that are critical to woman's identity and beingness. *In Praise of Virtue* addresses these issues while exploring the biblical virtues and their significance for everyone in the believing community, male and female.

Beyond the seminary classroom and the feminist critique, other audiences and interests have guided this study. It is hoped that leaders and educators in the church, both laity and clergy, and the men and women committed to spiritual renewal and the raising of social-consciousness will find this book useful and stimulating. Lastly, all those in other traditions who have long maintained an interest in the virtues and in their universal importance

are invited to peruse this book. One thinks, in particular, of the
Roman Catholic community, whose theologians have mined the
classical and theological virtues for years, and of the Jewish community with its rabbinic emphasis on Torah.

CHAPTER ONE

Virtue and the Virtues

Introduction

FOR THE PAST several decades Catholic and Protestant theologians alike have explored and developed theologies of virtue.[1] At the same time, they have critiqued and debated the value of these theologies and their proper role in and influence on the Christian life. They have also applied their theologies of virtue to the major faith-and-life issues of the day.

This interest in virtue has stemmed from the conviction that Christian character and our moral dispositions and habits are as important as any Christian statement of faith. That is, who a believer is and what a believer does or becomes is as important as any faith-claim a believer makes.

All told, this has been a welcomed trend. However, no one has identified the full range of biblical virtues that support such an interest. Nonetheless, the emphasis on virtue and the deepening of one's moral character has been applauded by a wide range of Christian theologians. Even in rabbinical and Torah studies a plethora of books related to this interest have appeared.[2]

1. See the "Selected Bibliography" at the end of this volume.
2. In particular, one thinks of Jacob Neusner's many works devoted to this context, especially his *Invitation to the Talmud: A Teaching Book* (New York: Harper & Row, 1973, expanded 1984), or of Judah Goldin's helpful *The Living Talmud* (1955) and its many reprints.

1

Some theologians caution that a renewed interest in virtue and moral character has the capacity to undo — at least for Protestants — the doctrine of salvation by grace through faith.[3] They fear that in the place of grace old levels of "works-righteousness" will re-emerge.

Since the time of the Hebrew prophets and especially since Augustine's struggle against the Donatists, theologians have warned that pride in one's personal virtues leads to attitudes and actions that are morally counterproductive. In modern times, both Nietzsche and Reinhold Niebuhr have warned of the powers of self-delusion, especially at a moral and spiritual level. Nietzsche's devastating analysis of the "priestly" doctrine of *ressentiment,* a doctrine based on the vengefulness and hatred of the weak for the strong, and Reinhold Niebuhr's exposure of "religious pride" as characterized by blindness to its own self-righteousness, are prime examples of such admonitions.

We ought also to acknowledge the feminist criticism of the traditionalist past and the way in which tradition has interpreted the human condition. To many feminists, "hierarchical" and "authoritarian" ideas have determined a general attitude toward women and women's uniqueness, which has not only led to the subjugation of women and the orders of nature but has robbed men of an adequate vision of their own wholeness. Any rethinking of virtue, therefore, should recognize the feminist idea of feminine experience and its importance to our understanding of human development and character.[4]

The truth of the matter is, however, that neither Catholics

3. See especially Gilbert Meilaender, *The Theory and Practice of Virtue* (Notre Dame, Ind.: University of Notre Dame Press, 1984). So also, Donald G. Bloesch, *Freedom For Obedience: Evangelical Ethics in Contemporary Times* (San Francisco: Harper & Row, Publishers, 1987). Bloesch warns: "Evangelical Christianity does not denigrate the life of virtue, but it insists that virtue is not enough. . . . Christians . . . are called not simply to a life of virtue but to a life that transcends virtue. . . . It is possible to speak of Christian virtue but always as something incomplete and deficient," 82.

4. For a helpful introduction to feminist theology, see Carol P. Priest and Judith Plaskow's *Womanspirit Rising: A Feminist Reader in Religion* (San Francisco: HarperSanFrancisco, 1992).

nor Protestants have sought to erode Christianity's historical doctrine of salvation by grace. Nor has either sought to detract from the validity of the feminist understanding of humankind's development or potential for moral virtue. Certainly, neither has wished to redefine the "holiness of the church" in terms of the "purity" of its members. On the contrary, what has impelled the theologians involved has been an interest in the Christian life itself. They understand the Christian life to be a matter of living out the call to become a child of God in unity with all God's children — male and female; of fully developing our humanity as persons created in the image of God, and, above all, of becoming the new being that Christ's death and resurrection make possible. This realization that the virtues, when properly captive to the work of the Holy Spirit, both flow from and deepen our inner character and renew our commitment to neighbor has revived an interest in the subject.

The Bible clearly lends its support to this cause. Although it has not been, and may not be, possible to develop a single, general, biblical theory of human good with which everyone would concur, there are biblical motifs that justify a reappraisal of an ethics of character, as well as material from which to infer a set of biblical virtues. It must be acknowledged, however, that this interest in virtue is more a phenomenon of Christianity's respect for the rational traditions of Western philosophy, than it is a movement indigenous to the soil of either the Hebrew Bible or the New Testament. Throughout the Bible, one truth reigns supreme that provides the fundamental metaphysics of any biblical ethics of character: *no one is saved by exercising virtue; nor is anyone damned for the lack of it. God and God's grace come first.* Only then can everything else be seen in its proper perspective — from the human response of faith, hope, and love, to the value of the classical virtues with their capacity to deepen personhood and mold character. As long as this order is preserved, human life ceases to be, contrary to Sartre's dictum, a "useless passion," and becomes a wonder, and we as creatures, "a little lower than God" (Ps. 8:5).

Toward a General Biblical Theory
of Good and Ethics of Character

A biblical ethics of character is possible only if founded on the biblical emphasis of God's initiative, wherein God chooses to create human life and summons that life to seek its highest fulfillment in the Divine. This teleological or ends-oriented view of human good is justified with the proviso that the ethical foundation of human life is God's interest in that life and what becomes of it, not our interest in our own life or what we can do, or what God can do for us, to enhance humankind. In the divine decision to create human beings, there emerges an implicit acknowledgment of God's stamp of value on and God's hope and esteem for each human life. What becomes of it, its development and end, is lovingly and jealously sought and watched over by the Creator-God. It is this focal point of grace that provides virtue and character with their theological grounds and makes them worthy of interest.[5]

The biblical story of creation, with its emphasis on our being created in the "image of God," being molded as male from the "dust of the earth" and as female from "the rib" of her partner, and on our first parents' encounter with the tree of the knowledge of good and evil, provides a substantive foundation for Christian theology to infer God's interest in human good and moral development. This does not imply that either human good or moral development is an end in itself to be pursued apart from God. In the Hebrew Bible, neither potentiality is viable. Nor can either stand on its own, independent of the Creator-Redeemer. Nonetheless God's interest in human good and moral development is symbolized in profound ways, as early as the oldest Hebrew traditions, in both the Priestly and Yahwist accounts of creation.

The matter of the *imago Dei,* or the Priestly vision of the creation of humanity in the *image of God,* should be considered

---

5. The matter of God's preceding grace, as foundational for all biblical ethics, is especially championed by Stephen C. Mott, *Biblical Ethics and Social Change* (New York: Oxford University Press, 1982), 22-38.

in two aspects: (1) the high human potential for intellectual development and moral sensitivity,[6] (2) the uniquely human capacity for fellowship and cooperation with God and neighbor.[7] It is these capacities, made possible by God, that underlie human interpersonal relationships and moral awareness.

According to the biblical tradition, God created humankind in "the image of God," after the divine "likeness," and placed them in positions of accountability and authority over all else in the created order. God created them "male and female" for their own completion, joy, and reciprocity with each other, then blessed and declared both them and this ordering sound.

This metaphor of "image" is vital to any biblical understanding of an ethics of character. On the one hand, it affirms the uniqueness of human beings, both male and female, as creatures endowed with great rational and moral capacities, emotional and relational gifts, which pertain to all humanity and which God has willed. From the time of Augustine to that of Reinhold Niebuhr, concepts of self-transcendence, self-expression, self-accountability, and self-determination have been associated with the idea of the "image of God."

According to the Hebrew Bible, the Fall resulted in humankind's alienation from God and in the loss of each person's moral capacity to stand innocent before God, self, and neighbor. From the traditionalist (Augustinian–Niebuhrian) point of view, human beings have become proud "sinners," insistent on charting their individual courses of action and now affected by the universal consequence of everyone doing the same. Accordingly, humankind's very rational powers are enwebbed in a pervasive self-orientation that affects the profoundest dimensions of our being, resulting, at a corresponding level, in self-promotion.

To this the feminist movement adds its own nuance. In the feminist critique, pride and guilt are the traditional forms of male anxiety, suited to the "masculine experience" of "assertiveness,

6. This motif is frequently cited as an Irenaean theme. See Irenaeus, *Against Heresies*, Bk. IV, Chaps. 37 & 38.

7. See Karl Barth's development of this theme in *Church Dogmatics*, Vol. III, Pt. I, Chap. IX, 40, 2.

becoming, and transcendence." In the "feminine experience" a different set of "fallen" characteristics obtain because, as the feminist critique maintains, woman's essential human nature is different from man's. If woman's basic structure is fundamentally other than man's, then the Fall involves far more than mere "pride" and "will-to-power." For woman's temptations, as one feminist theologian explains

> are better suggested by such items as triviality, distractibility, and diffusness; lack of an organizing center or focus; dependence on others for one's own self-definition; . . . sentimentality, . . . and mistrust of reason.[8]

Whether one is male or female, however, a close reading of the Scriptures reveals that its writers never saw the Fall as eroding God's "image" in either the male or the female to the extent that we cease to be capable of intellectual or moral activity, or relational and emotional responses. On the contrary, men and women alike are capable of impressive moral and intellectual achievements. The Scriptures maintain, not that we have lost our ability to act rationally or morally, but that we have lost our capacity to act free of pride and guilt, or without triviality and distraction, though not, of course, our capacity to think and act. This is Calvin's own position in the *Institutes* (2,1,8-11), where he deplores a fallen humanity's estimate of its rational powers, dignity, and morality. Nonetheless, he encourages all to love and pursue the arts and the sciences as well as to care about the civil order. Above all, he invites the redeemed to venture the Christian life, precisely because they have been redeemed by grace and are now in the process of having their true image "restored," thanks to the indwelling power of God.

The metaphor of the "image" is also important because it affirms human accountability before God and neighbor. The stories in Genesis make it clear that God loves humankind too much to indulge the human creature's moral despair or self-destruction. Though "fallen," we are still intelligent and moral beings and as

---

8. Valerie Saiving, "The Human Situation: A Feminine View," in *Womanspirit Rising*, 37.

humans are still responsible for our activities and attitudes. We remain accountable for their choices and their consequences and are answerable for the path each has elected and followed.

Not only is the biblical story careful not to denigrate a person's moral or intellectual capacities, but the Hebrew Bible presents God as refusing to absolve anyone of his or her personal accountability. Genesis 3–11 make it transparent that Adam and Eve, Cain, the entire generation of Noah, and the builders of the Tower of Babel (i.e., all of the archetypal figures) were capable of higher ends than their pride or self-indulgence, triviality or sentimentality, inspired them to attain. God expected more and refused to accept less. Rather, what the Bible emphasizes is the inadequacy of the human effort to repair the debilitating effects of pride and diffuseness, or sin and failure. Nothing humans do can make them "better" or "pure." Only God's love and grace can do that. Nonetheless, each is still an intelligent and moral being, capable of self-transcendence, self-expression, accountability, and self-determination. Above all, each is a being whom God loves and calls, forgives and regenerates, in order that each may become all that God desires for him or her.

The metaphors of "dust" and "rib" are also vital to a biblical ethics of character. According to the Yahwist story, God created the being *atham* from the "dust" of the earth and his partner *'ishshah* from the man's "rib." As such, both owe their existence to a power beyond themselves. "Dust" and "rib" make them equals. There is no hierarchy here, certainly not in any ontological or moral sense. Each is a creation of God's will, activity, and design. Still, however noble their status among the created goods of God's garden, as human beings they are derived from "dust" and "rib" — finite and mortal, limited by space and time and by all the contingencies of existence. They are creatures not gods. They are not those Dionysian, sovereign individuals, meant to determine their own destinies in defiance of God, whom Nietzsche longed for his *Ubermenschen,* or Overmen, to become. Their noblest achievements will always fall short of the God's highest hopes — no matter how brilliant, altruistic, and compassionate their efforts and attitudes may be.

This insight prepares the way for the third "metaphor" in

the Genesis story. In order to attain their end as caretakers of the planet and to fulfill their need for intimacy, partnership, love, and reciprocity, God provided the archetypal couple with each other and with a world teeming with life and beauty. And at the precise center of that order, at the heart of all that makes for humanness, God confronted the biblical couple with a phenomenon of the Divine's wisdom and love — the tree of the knowledge of good and evil. As such, the tree required the acknowledgment of and reflection on the only source of illumination and joy that sustains and nurtures human action and authentic personal development. To acknowledge this is to realize that only the life-giving Creator-God can and does provide the highest reason for human existence and the norm for all humankind's choices and actions. Otherwise, the end *(telos)*, or good of human existence, which is fellowship and reciprocity with God and neighbor, becomes unattainable as the stories in Genesis 3–11 attest.

One may ask, "How does virtue fit into any of this, if it does?"

For the Catholic existentialist, Romano Guardini, virtue "extends through the whole of existence" and both "ascends to God" and "descends from Him." As such, virtue is a dimension of God's "good," and virtues themselves "living treasures, radiating from God." Thus, "every virtue is a diffraction of this infinitely rich simplicity upon a potentiality of man."[9] On this basis, Guardini argues for a "virtue of order," that begins with God and emanates downward and outward to embrace all of humankind. Guardini writes:

> There is a truth, a reality upon which every order of existence depends. It is the fact that God alone is 'God' and that man is his creature and image — that God is really God, not an anonymous principle of the universe, not a mere idea, not the mystery of existence, but He who is himself the real and living one, Lord and Creator — and man is His creature and is obliged to obey the supreme Lord.[10]

9. Romano Guardini, *The Virtues: On Forms of Moral Life,* trans. Stella Lange (Chicago: Henry Regnery Company, 1967), 6-8.

10. Ibid., 6.

Less problematic than Guardini's "emanationist" view, however, is Aristotle's view of ethics. If virtue (at least in the philosophical sense) is understood as an "activity of the soul," as Aristotle defines it, "in conformity with right reason," then biblical
virtue involves at least two foci. First, it is an activity of the whole
person (heart, mind, and soul) in response to the highest contemplation of God which, by God's grace, God makes possible
(whether the contemplative vision is given at Sinai or in the life,
death, and resurrection of Jesus). Secondly, the soul's activity includes as an inseparable corollary the highest contemplation of
neighbor that one is willing and able to act on. In the New
Testament, it is what Jesus meant when he said to the lawyer: "You
shall love the Lord your God with all your heart, and with all your
soul, and with all your mind. . . . And . . . You shall love your
neighbor as yourself" (Matt. 22:37-39). And in the Torah, it is
expressed in all the redemptive "statutes" and "ordinances" that
God revealed to Moses in the Covenant.

This is what in the Protestant tradition the Reformers meant
by the phrase *sola gloria Dei:* to "the glory of God alone." For
Calvin, the highest human end is very simple and clear: to glorify
God. Where God is glorified through God's redemptive grace, then
God's love for and influence on each human being will lift that
life to its highest possibility. Or in contemporary theological terms,
where the Divine becomes the focal point for human transcendence, or even despairing diffuseness, our humanness is deepened
and self-forfeiture embraced. Or, as in Luther's case (in *The Freedom of a Christian*), the power of the Christian life flows from
that "righteousness" and "freedom" that are founded on the gospel
and cross of Christ alone. God's love, God's grace made first, will
arouse and deepen our sense of self and mold our moral character.

In sum, virtue, in the biblical sense, involves a positive response to God, and to what God has set in motion, rather than
preoccupation with mere human achievement. It is an activity of
the whole being in conformity with its highest end, which is to
glorify God and is, in the teachings of Jesus as well as those of
the Torah, achieved by loving God and loving neighbor. When that
response is made, a virtuous life follows, for man and woman.
God desires this response because it is necessary to our develop-

ment as God's sons and daughters. This response will then influence moral character and the virtues that sustain it and are sustained by it. But it is never a matter of mere self-improvement. Rather, it is necessarily a matter of God's grace making it possible to deepen our humanness and its possibilities for good.

If this description is accurate, then the biblical virtues include all those positive responses, attitudes, and moral habits that flow from a life that is open to the redemptive presence of God. That is to say, they include those responses of the whole person by which, as God's children, we are assisted to become fully what the Divine intended us to be when God created us in the divine image. As creatures in God's image, our end is to know and serve the Divine and to honor and love one another. To achieve that end, we were given a high potential for intellectual development, moral sensitivity, and loving reciprocity.

In the Jewish tradition, that end is possible because of God's gracious gift in the life-directing power of Torah. In the Christian tradition, however, it is possible only because of God's gracious action in the life, death, and resurrection of Jesus Christ, and because of the power of the Holy Spirit working within the believer. It cannot be attained apart from the activity of divine grace. For on one's own, without God's grace, we do not seek the end for which God has created us. As representatives of the human condition, the archetypal couple, prompted by both pride and passivity, chose not to seek their highest end; and humankind since has universally followed their lead. Until delivered from the morass of pride and guilt, or distractibility and loss of self-awareness, we continue to fall short of what God intended for us. We thus remain either victims of self-satisfied accomplishments, deluded by pride and our own ideologies, or become victimized by the delusions, selfishness, and unjust acts of others.

At the head of any biblical list of virtues comes *faith,* faith as trust in and loving commitment to the God of grace. This is what acknowledging one's self-understanding as a being created in the image of God presupposes and what accepting God as the author of moral good requires one to accept. Faith and obedience direct men and women toward their highest end, because faith focuses on the only power that can keep one's self-understanding and God-willed renewal on track. Only the love and power of God can sustain, preserve, and ultimately further the highest human ordering. In the Jewish tradition, this grace and power are inseparable from Torah. In the Christian faith, Christ's death, through God's power, delivers one from every vain and impossible attempt to secure that highest end for oneself. Faith in God is the virtue that promotes and directs all the God-given capacities for one's highest development and renewal as an intelligent, moral, and caring being. It holds humankind fast to the regenerating power of the Holy Spirit to renew us and all our relationships, both at the personal and communal level.

The point of this introduction, however, is only to establish the genuine possibility for a biblical ethics of virtue and character, which both the Hebrew Bible and the New Testament seem clearly to encourage believers to venture. The primary purpose of this book will be to explore the Bible for such an ethic, to identify the virtues and character-building motifs that the Bible extols, and to articulate them in a theologically accountable manner. Before beginning that exploration, however, there are antecedents from the classical age which deserve consideration. Likewise, there are medieval, modern, and contemporary views which also shed light on the subject and which we will consider throughout the book.

Philosophical Antecedents from the Classical Age

Although it was left to Aristotle to develop the most systematic treatment of an ethics of character, by the end of the fifth century B.C. the Greeks had already come to accept four virtues as significant because of their character-developing potential. They are wisdom, courage, temperance, and justice.

It was Plato who first best utilized them in *The Republic* in an effort to spell out the highest good that both an individual and the state can attain. When the rulers of a state wisely adopt the noblest of ends to be pursued by the state and its guardians courageously commit themselves to defending the state against its enemies within and without, and when its citizens, artisans, and craftsmen pursue their own trades with disciplined effort, then is justice, or the best ordering of the state, achieved. So also with the individual. When he or she wisely follows the noblest dictates of reason, courageously pursues them, while avoiding the distractions of self-indulgence, the well-ordering of the self becomes possible.

Few have expressed all this as powerfully as Guardini:

> There is one thing . . . that Plato's philosophy has made clear once for all; that is, after the confusion and chaos introduced into thought by the Sophists, he showed that absolute values exist, that these can be known, and that therefore there is such a thing as truth. He likewise showed that these values are summed up in the majesty of that which we call 'the Good,' and that this good can be realized in the life of man according to the potentialities of each individual. Plato showed that the good is identical with the divine; but that its realization leads man to true humanity, as virtue comes into being, and this virtue signifies perfection of life, freedom and beauty.[11]

It is Aristotle, however, who constructed the first philosophy of ethics around the virtues and explored the value of their character-molding potential.[12]

According to Aristotle, everything may be said to exist for some purpose, which is the "good" of that thing or end (Aristotle, 3). The highest end for human beings is happiness, but it is a happiness that only the noblest moral and intellectual effort can attain. Neither pleasure, wealth, honor, nor excellence can secure this happiness, as all these "goods" are not ends in themselves but rather means to a higher end and are dependent on fortune and outside agents. The highest human happiness can be attained only by the moral agent's own choices and efforts. Happiness, according to Aristotle, comes by one's own attempt to achieve life's highest satisfaction.

11. Ibid., from Preface, v.
12. Aristotle, *Nicomachean Ethics*, trans. Martin Oswald, The Library of Liberal Arts (New York: Macmillan Publishing Company, 1962). This translation of the *Nicomachean Ethics* is cited throughout.

Aristotle defines virtue as "an activity of the soul in conformity with right reason" (Aristotle, 17). But certain virtues are required to exercise right reason. These virtues consist of two kinds: intellectual and moral virtues. Intellectual virtues have to do with the attainment of truth, or with those methods that enable one to discern truth which requires both reasoning and desiring to be right. Intelligence must be motivated by desire and desire controlled by thought. The faculties by which the soul attains to right reason, according to Aristotle, are five: pure science, art, deliberation, intelligence, and theoretical wisdom, or a knowledge of the fundamental principles of life (Aristotle, 150). Knowledge of this last sphere sharpens human awareness of what truly makes human beings happy.

In contrast with the intellectual virtues, the moral virtues have to do with the human capacity to attain what right reason discerns. Hence, both the intellectual and moral virtues are required for happiness to be achieved. For Aristotle, moral virtue must put into action what the intellectual virtues grasp with clarity. But this takes commitment and action and the development of character. Hence, moral virtue has to do with acquiring the noblest human traits possible that govern "emotions" and "actions." As such, moral virtues enable the agent always to do the right thing at the right time for the right reason in the right way. It is something that one learns from habit and it requires years to perfect (if possible) or even to exercise well. As Aristotle puts it: "For one swallow does not make a spring, nor does one sunny day; similarly, one day or a short time does not make a man blessed and happy" (Aristotle, 17-18).

Virtue, Aristotle explains, requires choice, which requires reflection and intelligence. One must deliberate between alternatives. In order to attain the noblest ends, the noblest choices must be discerned, and once discerned, actualized or actually practiced. In other words, there can be no substitute for either personal decision-making or virtuous action. Both are necessary if the human soul is to fulfill its function according to its nature and attain its end. A high degree of self-determination and autonomy and personal accountability is therefore essential.

As Aristotle knew, behavior-building requires time. One's behavior is influenced over a long period of time as one becomes habituated to choosing the right ends for the right reasons and thus begins doing the right thing at the right time for the right purpose in the right manner. Each virtuous action reinforces the moral agent to venture the next virtuous action and so on. The whole process begins early in childhood, which is why Aristotle insists that pedagogy and education are so important. In one of his more poignant passages he observes: "For the things which we have to learn before we can do them we learn by doing; . . . men become just by the practice of just actions, self-controlled by exercising self-control; and courageous by performing acts of courage" (Aristotle, 34).

Since Aristotle took human emotions seriously and did not believe in repressing them, he realized that the right choice will always involve an appropriate degree of emotion in response to a specific situation, thus tempering one's final action. Aristotle developed this into a doctrine of the mean, whereby he sought the balance between overreacting and underreacting in any given situation. The median choice or mean between these two extremes becomes for Aristotle the proper virtue. As such, the mean choice avoids the excess on the one hand and its defect on the other. To act in either an excessive or a deficient manner is to fail to do the right thing for the right reason at the right time in the right way. The virtuous act expresses the mean.

A reading of Aristotle's *Nicomachean Ethics* enables us to reproduce something like the chart of virtues he apparently used with his students.

ARISTOTLE'S CHART OF VIRTUES

THE EXCESS	THE MEAN	THE DEFECT
Recklessness	Courage	Cowardice
Self-Indulgence	Self-Control	Insensitivity
Extravagance	Generosity	Stinginess
Vulgarity	Magnificence	Miserliness
Vanity	High-Mindedness	Small-Mindedness
Short-Temperedness	Gentleness	Apathy
Boastfulness	Truthfulness	Self-Deprecation
Buffoonery	Pleasantness	Boorishness
Obsequiousness	Friendliness	Grouchiness
Mortification	Shame	Shamelessness
Envy	Righteous Indignation	Spite

In the same book, Aristotle goes on to explore justice and friendship and the indispensable role each plays in developing character and creating the possibility for attaining happiness.

Considering that Aristotle precedes Christ by almost four centuries, his vision of the highest happiness humans can attain is a noble one. Although it cannot substitute for a biblical ethics of character and, of course, suffers from Aristotle's era's aristocratic and hierarchical notions, it still has much to offer by way of inspiration and instruction. Although its definition of humankind's highest end is limited, its concern for humanity's highest development and moral and intellectual "happiness" is on target. It represents a model against which the Christian faith can sharpen its own ideas and challenges believers to construct a corresponding chart of virtues appropriate to the biblical and Christian understanding of the highest human good. In that sense, it is a remarkable and valuable antecedent.

Aristotle's emphasis on accountability and acceptance for one's choice of direction in life deserves special praise. More so than Plato, he was aware of the powers of perversity and the fact that the will can become so disordered that it chooses the wrong action knowingly and helplessly. He would call it "moral weakness," but it foreshadows St. Paul's own indictment of the will: "I do not do what I want, but I do the very thing that I hate. . . . Wretched man that I am! Who will rescue me from this body of death?" (Rom. 7:15, 24).

Later the Stoics would pursue their own explorations of virtue. Epictetus, one of the school's more prolific writers, would build his ideas on a theme taken from Aristotle's understanding of "choice." Aristotle realized that no one can be deemed accountable if denied voluntary choice. But for choice to be voluntary, it must be within the agent's power to choose (Aristotle, 68). Epictetus adopts Aristotle's phrase, "in our power," and launches his own investigation of what leads to the highest human good.

Since he assumed that "will," "the emotions," and "self-control" are within one's power, Epictetus further developed the rather bleak, if not pessimistic, philosophy of Stoicism, which taught that virtue lay in enduring the things we have no power over rather than in actively pursuing a happy life according to the power we do have to achieve it. "We must make the best of those things that are in our power, and take the rest as nature gives it" — nature being deemed equivalent to God's will. But this leads to an accommodation with evils (viewed as beyond one's power) and introduces a morbid resignation toward, if not an inordinate fascination with, death, pain, and suffering.[13] "Never say of anything, 'I lost it,' but say, 'I gave it back.' . . . Has your wife died? She was given back. . . . What does it matter to you through whom the Giver asked it back?"[14] One can admire Epictetus's longing for a peace and serenity that transcends life's tragic dimensions, but his version of tranquillity is a nostrum and an attempt to escape the harrowing truth of one's humanness when severed from the power and grace of God.

Epictetus would also limit how much pleasure one ought to seek, contributing eventually to the unfortunate Christian inclination to embrace asceticism which Jesus himself never practiced as an end in itself.

Seneca, one of St. Paul's contemporaries, also extolled the virtue of self-denial. He addressed many letters to friends in which he discussed the virtues and argued that adversities are necessary if the highest human end is to be obtained. This is especially so in his

13. See *The Discourses of Epictetus* in *The Stoic and Epicurean Philosophers*, ed. Whitney J. Oates (New York: The Modern Library, 1940), 225.
14. Ibid., 470.

essay *On Providence,* in which he praises God for sending hardship, sorrows, and disasters, because by life's adversities our mettle can be proven and our moral character developed.[15] But that is hardly what the biblical virtues are about. Nor does that view embody the highest good God's creatures are capable of attaining. Not merely endurance, or self-realization, but reciprocity with God and neighbor are, from the biblical perspective, the ends for which men and women are created and which can be attained only by grace.

Aquinas's Theory of Virtue

It is a great leap from the Stoics of the classical period to the scholasticism of the Middle Ages, but for our purposes it is a leap we can justify. Aquinas's theory of character and the virtues is both similar to and yet different from Aristotle's. It is similar insofar as Aquinas adopts Aristotle's "eudaemonological and teleological standpoint,"[16] but it is unlike the latter's insofar as St. Thomas provides a different interpretation of happiness and of the virtues required to attain it.

For Aquinas, as for Aristotle, there is a proper and unique end for humankind to attain, a unique function which we were meant to serve. That end is happiness, but not the happiness based on the successful pursuit of the moral and intellectual virtues alone. As Aquinas explains, it is a twofold happiness.[17] The one is "imperfect" and attainable "in this life," the other is "perfect" and consists in the "vision of God" (I, 2, Q.4, A.5, 19:633). According

15. Seneca, *De Providentia,* in *Seneca: Moral Essays,* trans. John W. Basore, Loeb Classical Library (Cambridge: Harvard University Press, 1963), 9, 11, 15, 27, 29, 37-39.

16. See Frederick Copleston, *A History of Philosophy,* Vol. 2, Pt. II (New York: Image Books, 1962), 119.

17. Subsequent quotations from Aquinas are taken from Thomas Aquinas, *The Summa Theologia,* in *Great Books of the Western World,* Vols. 19 and 20 (Chicago: Encyclopaedia Britannica, Inc., 1952). Citations will be given parenthetically in the text and will refer to part number, question, answer, and volume and page numbers.

to St. Thomas, imperfect happiness can be acquired now, in this
life, by the exercise of our "natural powers"; but perfect happiness
requires God's assistance if the divine promise is ever to be realized,
and it will not be fully realized until after this life (I, 2, Q.5, A.5,
19:640).

Aquinas agrees with Aristotle that happiness is not to be
equated with wealth or honor, power or health or with any created
good. Only the highest *object* of contemplation and the highest
act of human *activity* can satisfy the highest end, which is both to
know and *love* God (I, 2, Q.2, As.1-8).

Aquinas further agrees with Aristotle that happiness is a kind
of activity or operation; it is the actualization of one's essential
nature as a human. As an act, it involves both the intellect and the
will. The two are inseparable. As Aquinas explains: "Every act of the
will is preceded by an act of the intellect, but a certain act of the will
precedes a certain act of the intellect" (I, 2, Q.4, A.4, 19:632). The
intellect is needed to know the highest end, but the will is required
to support and move the intellect toward that high end, or toward
the object of its contemplation. It is what Jesus meant, Aquinas
suggests, when Christ said, "Blessed are the pure in heart, for they
shall see God" (Matt. 5:8). Here the will and the highest end that the
intellect can know are wedded. Once the intellect has informed the
will of the desired end, then the will, willing that end, is free to will
the means to attain it (I, 2, Q.9, A.3, 19:659). This eventually brings
Aquinas to a discussion of the virtues.

At this juncture, Aquinas once again takes Aristotle's lead by
calling virtue a habit. Habits imply "dispositions" and "opera-
tions," but which must be in proportion to the end or goal. When
an act is based on a right disposition, then that act enables us as
moral agents to fulfill our end. Hence, habits are necessary for the
"perfection of ends" (I, 2, Q.49, A.4, 20:5). Since "like habits cause
like ends," they can be increased as easily as diminished. It all
depends on the will (I, 2, Q.52, A.3, 20:19).

Virtues develop, then, as forms of habits. When habits are
virtuous they dispose us more permanently toward our highest end
(I, 2, Q.55, A.1, 20:26). Thus virtues, as "operating habits," contribute to an agent's highest end. They "make" the "subject good"
(I, 2, Q.55, A.3, 20:28). They render both the possessor and his

or her work good (I, 2, Q.56, A.3, 20:31). (Notice in this system that virtues can make a person "better and better.")

Also in accordance with Aristotle, Aquinas designates the virtues as either "intellectual" or "moral." The moral pertain to the "appetitive" side of human nature and the intellectual to the rational (I, 2, Q.56, A.5, 20:33). When the appetitive side of humanness, the "irascible and concupsicible powers," are governed by reason, then courage and temperance result (I, 2, Q.56, A.6, 20:34).

Wisdom, or prudence, on the other hand, is an intellectual virtue. For St. Thomas, it is the most important of the four cardinal virtues. It is the "most necessary for human life" (I, 2, Q.57, A.5, 20:39). Since a good life consists in doing good, and doing good requires both a disposition toward good actions and the good done rightly, then a person must understand both the end toward which all his or her action is directed as well as the means for attaining that end. "Consequently an intellectual virtue is needed in the reason, to perfect the reason, and make it suitably disposed toward things ordered to the end; and this virtue is prudence" (I, 2, Q.57, A.5, 20:39). Reason, then, is the "first principle of all human acts" and lies behind all other principles of human action.

As wisdom guides the intellect, so the moral virtues guide and control the human appetites. Thus the intellectual virtues perfect the reason. As such, they are prior to the moral virtues and independent of them, that is, the moral virtues could not exist without the intellectual, which guide all dispositions and actions (I, 2, Q.58, As.2-5, 20:42-45).

Aquinas also follows Aristotle's lead in making the virtues the mean choices and acts between emotions and actions. In particular, the moral virtues perfect the appetitive in human nature and bring it into conformity with reason. But Aquinas goes beyond Aristotle and grounds all the virtues in the Godhead: They, says Aquinas, "pre-exist in God as exemplars." *Wisdom* is the Divine Mind; *temperance* is God gazing "only on Himself"; *courage is* God's "unchangeableness"; and *justice is* God's "obedience of the Eternal Law" (I, 2, Q.61, A.5, 20:59).

The importance of Aquinas's insight here cannot be over estimated. What it suggests is that wherever wisdom, temperance, courage, and justice surface in human acts and dispositions, there, to the extent that they genuinely appear, God is present. God the highest good and the highest actuality is present in human experience, and to that extent, we can enjoy happiness in this life though imperfectly. God is here, in our midst, seeking and caring about humanity, lifting it, at least to the extent that traces of "the image of God" are still morally and intellectually active in it, toward its highest good. That is the basis of every moral philosophy and the foundation for its universality. For it both witnesses to the echo of God's "image" in every human being and possesses the power to keep human relationships human.

If anyone is uneasy with this idea of the virtues having their source in God, it would be feminists, who are concerned that grounding these "masculine virtues" so ardently as "exemplars" in God only intensifies that unwholesome bifurcation between Spirit and Nature, Mind and Body, which feminists find questionable and foreign to feminine experience. Nonetheless, for Aquinas, men and women are designed for a greater happiness than promised by any merely human ethos. They are meant to attain to a happiness in conformity with their highest end, which is to know, love, and see God. Thus Aquinas ushers in the theological virtues of faith, hope, and charity.

Aquinas begins his section on the theological virtues by reminding his readers of the twofold nature of happiness: the one proportionate to human nature and its principles, the other surpassing it and requiring the "power of God alone, by a kind of participation of the Godhead" (I, 2, Q.62, A.1, 20:60). The natural principles are simply insufficient to direct human beings to their "supernatural happiness," hence higher principles are required. These are the principles Aquinas chose to call the theological virtues. They are called theological, "first, because their object is God and direct us rightly to God; secondly, because they are infused in us by God alone; and thirdly, because these virtues are not known to be except by Divine revelation" (I, 2, Q.62, A.1, 20:60). As such they illuminate the human reason and motivate the will toward the good. They bring about "the rectitude of the will" that it may engage in true acts of charity (I, 2, Q.62, A.3, 20:61).

In the order of the theological virtues, faith precedes hope and hope charity. But in the order of their "perfection," charity precedes both faith and hope and perfects them as virtues (I, 2, Q.62, A.4, 20:62).

In the same way, human reason, or Aristotle's right reason, illumines the will to act in fulfillment of one's natural happiness, for Aquinas the Divine Law illumines the human will to act in fulfillment of its supernatural happiness. But this latter capacity is "produced in us by the Divine operation alone" through the "infused virtues" of faith, hope, and charity (I, 2, Q.63, A.2, 20:64).

These "infused virtues" are necessary and differ significantly from "acquired virtues." Only the infused virtues are perfect, for they alone are able to direct us toward our ultimate end in the vision of God. Nevertheless, the acquired virtues are not without merit, for they also direct humankind in a "particular genus of action" (I, 2, Q.65, A.2, 20:72). But for Aquinas, the love and goodness of God is mirrored in all the moral virtues, because each represents a form of good, and God is the highest good. Thus, even a "natural man," living in conformity with right reason, would still be a witness to the high intellectual and moral capacities with which God has endowed him, thus reflecting God's care for him and longing for him to obtain life's highest satisfaction. This is biblical, because it underscores God's hope and love for each human being and God's desire that one's whole life be anchored in the Divine.

Nietzsche and the Modern Era

We turn briefly to Friedrich Wilhelm Nietzsche, because any serious study of the Bible's ethics of character ought willingly to hear Nietzsche out, or, at least, be willing to consider his complaint.

Nietzsche acknowledges that early in his youth Christianity became less and less attractive while his forays into the study of Greek culture became increasingly addictive. There he encountered what he would call a clash between the Apollinian and the Dionysian motifs that he supposed underlie all human thought and action.[18]

18. Friedrich Nietzsche, *The Birth of Tragedy*, trans. Walter Kaufmann (New York: Vintage Books, 1967), 33-60 in particular.

By the Apollinian motif he meant all that illumines and gives order and structure to life; by the Dionysian he meant all that is dark, primordial, unstructured, dynamic, at pain with itself, yet creative. Historically, Nietzsche claims, the Apollinian motif won out — as represented by Socrates and Plato who opted for order, reason, and virtue; but it did so at the expense of mystery and freedom. They proposed a system of values that extolled being, goodness, and truth, but which did so in abstract and formal ways, which repressed the darker and unbounded urges of what is equally "human," "good," and "true." Thus the Apollinian motif led to a metaphysics, that is to systems of being and value, that impact with as much bondage and untruthfulness as with liberation and order. To get behind these values, as well as the virtues they spawn, became Nietzsche's chief obsession.

Nietzsche would label this obsession a desire to "revaluate all values."[19] Since he had ceased to believe in God or in any absolute determiner of values, he turned to the self, to the Dionysian nature within, to find a new center for determining all values. Coupling this turn with an interest to fathom the origin of values, Nietzsche concluded that the "good" is not so much the result of what "unegoistic actions" produce, but rather what the "high-minded," the "noble," the "powerful," and the "aristocratic" of the earliest societies determined was "good" (*Genealogy*, 26). These noble, "blond beasts," were warriors whose own values had been forged in their long history of struggle, pain, blood, and cruelty. They were values that had come out of years of suffering and strife.

A "priestly caste" eventually came to power in many societies and with its emergence appeared a new set of values. "Good" and "bad" now became defined in terms of "pure" and "impure" (*Genealogy*, 31). In time, these societies gave birth to values that were "antithetical" to the values of the noble caste; these new values became increasingly internalized, morbid, and unhealthy. Indeed, "with the priests, *everything* becomes more dangerous," says Nietzsche, even their "arrogance, revenge, acuteness, profligacy, love, lust to rule, virtue, disease" (*Genealogy*, 32). Ultimately,

19. See *"On the Genealogy of Morals" and "Ecce Homo,"* trans. Walter Kaufmann (New York: Vintage Books, 1989), 326.

it was this ethic that gave birth to the tragic morality of *"ressenti-ment"* — a morality that reverses the noble virtues of the "blond beast" in favor of virtues that, out of hate and vengeance, extol meekness, submission, God, the soul, and the hereafter (*Genealogy,* 33-36 and passim).

As a further consequence, "guilt" and "bad conscience" became associated with violating the values of the priestly caste and led to an even greater reversal of values. The repression of one's Dionysian nature only exacerbated one's sense of guilt and gave the priestly element still greater power. Hence, much of what is defined as true, good, and virtuous is, on the contrary, only the scraps of a sickly, unhealthy interpretation of "good" and "bad."

The greatest evil which Nietzche feared in all of this is that humankind will succumb to *nausea* and *pity,* terms which for Nietzsche imply defeatism and nihilism (*Genealogy,* 122). Labeling the priests the "greatest haters" of the world, Nietzsche feared humankind would accept a "leveling" and "diminution" of the self, an acquiescence that would lead to despair and self-pity. Nietzsche believed that to prevent this tragic "fall" of humankind a new moral power and center was necessary that makes human beings gods in themselves.

Nietzsche would flesh this out in the form of his *Ubermensch.* The *Ubermensch,* or overman, represents for Nietzsche the kind of Dionysian person one must become. Such a person is a "sovereign individual," who becomes one's own center of good and evil in conflict and reciprocity with other sovereign individuals. Only this person is "liberated" from the "morality of custom." Only this soul can be "autonomous and supramoral," "the man who has his own independent, protracted will," "a proud consciousness of his own power and freedom" (*Genealogy,* 59). Only this person can then posit the values and virtues that are needed to save humankind from "nausea" and "pity."

But what is the meaning of such a life? What is its ultimate end, its highest goal, its greatest "good"? Indeed, can there be one? Yes, Nietzsche replies, but this "Yes-saying" to life can come about only after great struggle, only after one passes beyond the "death of God" and the "twilight of idols." The clearing of the "fossils" of the mind comes about only with great effort.

In an essay devoted to the "ascetic ideal," Nietzsche realized that one cannot remain human without searching for some "release from . . . torture" (*Genealogy*, 106). Therefore humankind has perennially sought an ascetic ideal "as an expression of the basic fact of the human will," which is its "horror of a vacuum," its need of a goal (*Genealogy*, 97). But to achieve this goal requires independence and the need to affirm one's existence. It requires a return to the *desert*, with all its austere and cleansing powers. In the long run, human beings so need to fill this void, to grasp the goal, to deal with meaning, that they will rather "will *nothingness* than *not* will" at all (*Genealogy*, 163).

In the last book he wrote, before his mind disintegrated and he entered into the long shadow of insanity, he ended his search with this sudden and defiant line: "Have I been understood? — Dionysus versus the Crucified" (*Genealogy*, 335).

Nietzsche once said of himself that his destiny was to be the first "decent man," the first to judge the Christian morality as "beneath" him. One must not mitigate Nietzsche's sense of purpose or attempt to trivialize or dismiss his attack on Christian morality as being unfair, wrong, or the rantings of a tragic maniac or misguided male. The truth of Nietzsche's attack on a morality of *ressentiment* stands on its own merits — then and now. His desire for values and virtues to be founded on strength and not weakness, on the best and "noblest" in human beings rather than on the worst and most vengeful, should wrest a modern era's praises, not its hoots or curses. Above all, he makes clear what an ethic of character will mean if God is denied and where humankind chooses to magnify its "dignity" in defiance of its equally natural limitations. But that only underscores the truth of the biblical vision of what alone can guarantee human happiness. Even more his concern that humankind not fall into what he called "nausea" or "pity" equally bears witness to God's own highest hopes for all, that each becomes anew what the Divine has created each forever to be: a man or woman created in God's "image" with incredible potential for partnership and reciprocity with the Divine and one another.

Stanley Hauerwas

Among Protestants, perhaps no contemporary theologian has inspired as great an interest in an ethics of character as Stanley Hauerwas. The catalyst for the occasion has been his doctoral dissertation: *Character and the Christian Life: A Study in Theological Ethics*.[20] Published in 1975, it continues to attract both praise and debate.

For Hauerwas the moral life consists in more than simply making rational choices. His central thesis is that an agent's character is inseparable from his or her self-determination and that the virtues, if they are to be rightly understood, are subordinate to character. He writes: "By the idea of character I mean the qualification of man's self-agency through his beliefs, intentions, and actions, by which a man acquires a moral history befitting his nature as a self-determining being" (*Character*, 11). To attribute character to a person is, thus, to attribute some level of self-control and self-mastery to a person in his or her efforts to regulate dispositions and actions. Consequently, character means that we are more than what simply happens to us. For a person "has the capacity to determine himself beyond momentary excitations and acts" (*Character*, 15).

Virtue, then, is subordinate to character. Virtue requires effort; but even so, any virtue's particular form will be determined by character. Character is therefore fundamental. Moreover, since we are "autonomous centers of activity," it is not so much that our volitions, motives, intentions, and reasons cause us to act, but rather that, as self-determining beings, we embody them.

To reinforce this insight, Hauerwas turns first to Aristotle and then to Aquinas to demonstrate that even their systems contain this distinction.

For Aristotle, Hauerwas notes, the primary focus of ethics is how an agent becomes good or bad through his activity. A person

20. Stanley Hauerwas, *Character and the Christian Life: A Study in Theological Ethics* (San Antonio: Trinity Press, 1975). See also Hauerwas, *Vision and Virtue: Essays in Christian Ethical Reflection* (Notre Dame: Fides Publishers, Inc., 1974), 48-67.

is the source or cause of his or her own actions. There may be
reasons for our choices, but, as free moral agents, we determine
both our choices and the kind of persons we become. Reason may
tell us what to do, but "for an act to be good it must be the result
of our character, for our character is the locus of the beliefs and
descriptions" through which we perceive our obligations (*Character*, 61). Hauerwas explains: "Aristotle knew very well that character implies more than a man's knowing what is right" for the
"self acquires character only through activity and by a long and
gradual growth" (*Character*, 68). Thus in Aristotle's scheme, for
a person to have character he or she must in turn acquire certain
habits, which are called virtues.

The virtues, then, are forms of readiness to act in specific
ways, habits formed by activity. In their widest meaning, they are
"that which causes a thing to perform its function well." Nonetheless, the "primary function of man is to act and in so doing
form himself by deliberative reason. Thus the man of virtue
is formed by repeated acts of deliberative decisions" (*Character*,
71).

For Aristotle, notes Hauerwas, there are finally three means
by which persons become good and virtuous: "the natural endow-
ments we have at birth; the habits we form; and the rational
principle within us" (*Character*, 77). Thus, even for Aristotle, the
virtues are best thought of as "skills for action" by which the
autonomous person shapes himself or herself toward life's highest
end.

As for Aquinas, Hauerwas deems him to have followed a
similar path. Because men and women are rational natures, they
possess "the capacity to be directly and ultimately the source of . . .
[their] own determinations" (*Character*, 62). Being and doing are
inseparable. Hence the virtues become "operative habits" which
determine an agent's end and perfection (*Character*, 79). But in
the final analysis, notes Hauerwas, according to Aquinas no virtue
can be true that is not ordered by charity — as we have already
seen.

Thus Hauerwas returns to his theme: as free moral agents,
what we do is more intimately related to what we become than a
cause is to an effect. And character, again, is the decisive factor

behind what we do and who we become. "Character is not just the sum of all that we do as agents, but rather it is the particular direction our agency acquires by choosing to act in some ways rather than others" (*Character*, 117). Thus character is molded as much by intentions and beliefs as by acts themselves. Our moral career is therefore as rich or impoverished as we choose to make it.

Having explored the phenomenon of character, Hauerwas now turns to relate it to the Christian life. For the Christian, character is inseparable from justification and sanctification. For Hauerwas, God's command, as expressed in the Decalogue and elsewhere, is given not merely to mold specific actions and intentions, but is given as both judgment and forgiveness. It comes as judgment, "because the self has a duration that allows for growth and development." But at the same time, it comes as forgiveness, "because we can do nothing to change our past, but we are not condemned to repeat it" (*Character*, 178).This is what our examination of the early Genesis stories confirmed.

For Hauerwas, apart from a response to Jesus Christ, adherence to virtues cannot produce a Christian life. Justification and sanctification must be held together. With Calvin, Hauerwas agrees:

> The whole may be summed up: Christ, given to us by the kindness of God, is apprehended and possessed by faith by means of which we obtain in particular a twofold benefit; first, being reconciled by the righteousness of Christ, God becomes instead of a judge an indulgent Father; and, secondly, being sanctified by His Spirit, we aspire to integrity and purity of life. (*Inst.* 3.11.1)[21]

In Hauerwas's view, the pursuit of a virtuous life is impossible if severed from sanctification. Sanctification is never simply a program of dispositions and actions, but rather it is "the effect of the conformation of the self to God's act" in Christ (*Character*, 191). Outward conduct must always be accompanied by an inward reformation of the heart.

21. See Hauerwas's discussion of Calvin, *Character*, 184-96.

Hauerwas sees a fourfold interconnection between sanctification and the virtuous life. Sanctification requires (1) that it be determined by a person's innermost being, (2) that it involve more than a single disposition or act, (3) that it involve our innermost dispositions and beliefs as well as our outward behavior, (4) that it result in the acknowledgment that our acts can conform to and reveal our intentions and beliefs (*Character,* 201-2).

Being and doing are one. In the final analysis, sanctification results in a life that is constantly reevaluating itself and its actions in light of God's sanctifying action within the believer and his community.

But Hauerwas warns of pride. Only the proud could be duped into believing that our moral actions make us better. The growth experienced in sanctification is not a matter of becoming "better and better." Rather, it is a "deepening of our self's determining" in the light of Christ's impact upon a believer's life, an impact in which Christ ever remains the center of the believer's "orientation and loyalty" (*Character,* 220).

Hauerwas's view is of great support, because, as we have seen, an ethics of character emphasizes, not one's becoming "better and better," but a "deepening of our self's determining" — to borrow Hauerwas's words. It stresses a "deepening" of potential as persons created with high intellectual and moral capacities, emotional and relational gifts, both for reciprocity with God and neighbor. This is why the virtuous life is worth living for Christians, because when it is made captive to God's love and grace, it becomes a means by which God deepens one's being and renews one's awareness of neighbor. Indeed, the old language of the *Westminster Confession of Faith*'s Chapter XIII, "On Sanctification," puts it quite well:

> I. They who are effectually called and regenerated, having a new heart and a new spirit created in them, are . . . sanctified . . . through the virtue of Christ's death and resurrection, by his Word and Spirit dwelling in them; the dominion of the whole body of sin is destroyed, and the several lusts thereof are more and more weakened and mortified, and they more and more quickened and strengthened, in all saving graces, to the practice of true holiness, without which no man shall see the Lord.

II. This sanctification is throughout in the whole man, yet imperfect is this life; there abideth still some remnants of corruption in every part, whence ariseth a continual and irreconcilable war, the flesh lusting against the spirit, and the spirit against the flesh.

III. In which war, although the remaining corruption for a time may much prevail, yet, through the continual supply of strength from the sanctifying Spirit of Christ, the regenerate part doth overcome; and so the saints grow in grace, perfecting holiness in the fear of God.

In spite of its quaintness, this is a clear affirmation of the meaning of the "image of God" and creation from "the dust of the earth" and the "rib" of the other. God has created men and women with high capacities both to know and do the right and to enjoy a reciprocity with the Divine and one another that fulfills God's highest hopes for all. But it cannot be attained aside from God's "sanctifying Spirit" and the "saving graces" of Christ. But where the self is redefined and indwelled by God, the "regenerate part doth overcome" and believers "grow in grace, perfecting" what God has willed for them to become.

On the basis of this introduction, we turn to the Bible to investigate its own ethics of character.

CHAPTER TWO

Exploring the Hebrew Bible's Ethics of Character: From the Earliest Genesis Stories to the Deuteronomic Torah

FOR LUTHER the presence of the Holy Spirit in a believer's life mitigates any need to be bound by the Old Testament's moral laws. The Spirit of Christ in one's heart is sufficient. For Luther the righteousness of Christ sweeps away all righteousness of works. Justification by grace through faith comes first; sanctification flows from it, without need of binding, moral directives. The preeminence of the cross controls all else. As Luther explains:

> But Christ, according to his true definition, is no lawgiver but a forgiver of sins and a saviour. . . .
>
> When we have thus taught faith in Christ, then do we teach also good works. Because thou hast laid hold upon Christ by faith, through whom thou art made righteous, begin now to work well. Love God and thy neighbor, call upon God, give thanks unto him, praise him, confess him. Do good to thy neighbor and serve him: fulfil thine office. These are good works indeed, which flow out of this faith and this cheerfulness conceived in the heart. . . .[1]

1. *A Commentary on St. Paul's Epistle to the Galatians* in *Martin Luther:*

Yet Luther loved the Psalms, David, Moses, and, above all, Abraham. He thought of the Psalms as containing God's love letters to Martin Luther and drew tremendous strength from Abraham as the embodiment of the true exemplar of faith. Commenting on Gen. 15:6 ("And Abraham believed God"), Luther writes:

> Abraham was a man who, at all times, was ready to believe God; he was always a believer. . . . So then: "Abraham believed God" means that he regarded God as truthful; and "to believe God" is as much to say "to believe him at all times and places."[2]

It is this faith in God then, in the saving power of God, that comes first for Luther, so much so as to eliminate reliance on everything else, certainly on any "works of the flesh," or on any sense of one's personal virtue or dignity. For Luther, the Old Testament, or any shades of good works it might teach, stands subservient to the New Testament's story of grace. Justification by faith first; only then comes sanctification. In Luther's view, this is the proper Christian ordering of the good life and the preamble for any exploration of the Hebrew Bible's virtues or interest in character. It is Luther's legacy to the Protestant tradition and has guided many Protestant interpretations since the Reformation.

Unlike Luther, Calvin was committed to the unity of the Scriptures and considered each of the Testaments to be morally and theologically valid. Calvin believed that the will of God is the same whether encountered in the Old Testament or the New. He also believed that, because Christ is the center of the whole Bible, both covenants promise eternal life and are founded on salvation by grace through faith. Thus Calvin felt empathetic toward much in the Hebrew Bible and could identify with both its themes and characters. He could understand their plights, needs, and hopes. Furthermore, he accepted the full, moral validity of the Decalogue, emphasizing its usefulness in the Christian life, and preached a

---

Selections from His Writings, ed. John Dillenberger (Garden City: Anchor Books, 1961), 110-12.

2. *Luther: Lecture on Romans,* trans. Wilhelm Pauck, Library of Christian Classics, Vol. XV (Philadelphia: Westminster Press, 1961), 122.

popular series of sermons on the subject, *Sermons on the Ten Commandments,* whose published English version alone enjoyed no less than six printings by 1581.[3] In addition, Calvin drew freely from the moral admonitions throughout the legal sections of the Pentateuch and applied them to both the Christian life and the political scene in Geneva.

Many scholars today draw a sharp distinction between the Hebrew Bible, with its unique theology, ethics, and worldview, and the New Testament, which they see as standing in relationship to, but not necessarily as the fulfillment of, the earlier books of the Bible. Modern scholarship is somewhat loathe to "read back into" the Hebrew Bible such Christian beliefs as either Calvin or Luther entertained.

For Christians, however — whether Protestant or Catholic — the Bible constitutes a unity of revelation and religious insight essential to the Christian life. The entire Bible is viewed as every Christian's spiritual heritage, somewhat like the Talmud is by orthodox Jews. It is his or her true spiritual home and, in spite of its acknowledged subordination of woman, is still filled with sound resources and insight concerning one's development as a person created in the image of God.

To help organize an exploration of the Hebrew Bible, five interrelated areas will be examined in this and the succeeding chapter: (1) the primeval history of the early Genesis stories, (2) the patriarchal sagas, (3) the legal materials of the Pentateuch, (4) the prophetic and historical books, and (5) the insight of the wisdom writers. From each of these resources, an attempt will be made to deduce those virtues and insights that, belonging to the Hebrew Bible, contribute to one's development as a human being. In many instances, the narrativist *quality* of this material will take center stage, along with the realization that narrativist *interests* guide its interpretation. By narrativist interests is meant the recognition that much of the Hebrew Bible is a profound historical-theological narrative, subservient to the theological views and intentions of the community which produced it and preserved it in

3. *John Calvin's Sermons on the Ten Commandments,* ed. and trans. Benjamin W. Farley (Grand Rapids: Baker Book House, 1980), 33.

distinct literary genres. This is especially true of the *saga* form of the patriarchal stories, versus the *"narrative-injunctions"* that preserve the Covenant and Torah, versus the longer *histories* of the Deuteronomistic writer or writers. Once each genre's guiding theological considerations are brought into focus, the "virtues" each piece of literature extols assume an appropriate validity.

The Early Genesis Stories

As indicated in Chapter One, Genesis chapters 1–3 provide ample insight for formulating a general, biblical theory of the good. From a contextual perspective, these stories of primeval history are comprised of Yahwist and Elohist traditions (J) and the views of the Priestly writers (P). Four themes emerge based on (1) God's creative, electing initiative (P), (2) humankind's subsequent creation in the "image of God" (P), (3) the male fashioned from the "dust of the earth" and the female from Adam's "rib" (J), and (4) both bounded by the phenomenon of the tree of the knowledge of good and evil (J & P).

The first has to do with God's nature, with the living God, who creates out of the profundity and mystery of love. Throughout the Bible, it is God's love and creative initiative that come first, that form the presupposition for everything else. It is God who initiates it all. It is God's grace that forms the foundation for all else. Accordingly, the creation of humankind marks a high and hopeful "moment" within the mystery of the divine will, because it reveals so clearly the depth of God's goodness and self-giving nature.

This means that the mystery and purpose of human creation lies in nothing less than God's unselfish and free decision to bring human life into being. God, who chose to share the divine splendor and glory with humankind, is humankind's Creator. Thus because the God of grace is our Creator and alone is life's highest good, human meaning and purpose are given a transcendent dimension. This emphasis on God's love, God's will, initiative, grace, and act, underlies the entire Genesis narrative. In doing so, it constitutes the foundation for humankind's highest hope and moral effort. It pervades every segment of the Hebrew Bible and all its traditions. It is the presupposition behind the sagas, the Israelite deliverance from bondage, God's faithfulness to Israel and Judah throughout their respective histories, and the central theme underlying the prophets' calls to repentance and newness of life. It is met repeatedly. Consequently, all human virtues are subordinate to the divine initiative and flow from a life that responds positively to God's grace and redemptive activity.

From a Christian perspective, it is this insight that constitutes the Christian's first principle. Once it is grasped, one can understand why Luther envisioned all of life as a *coram Deo*,[4] a life meant to be lived "before God," or "in the presence of God," and why Calvin wrote that "we are not our own, but belong to God."[5] Within this context, virtue and a virtuous life are given their true biblical foundation. This free, electing, creative initiative of God is what makes all else humans become and do intelligible and exciting.

The second theme is humanity's creation "in the image of God." This theme has already been developed in Chapter One, but its importance requires reiteration. In the Priestly account of creation (Gen. 1:1-31), "male and female" are together created in the "image of God." This passage is vital to human self-understanding and moral effort, because it acknowledges the equality of the sexes and their human uniqueness. It instructs us to understand that male and female together were created as equals and were endowed with immense intellectual and moral capacities, as well as emotional and relational abilities, for reciprocity and fellowship with God and one another. "Then God said, 'Let us make humankind in our image, according to our likeness. . . .' So God created humankind in his image, in the image of God he created them; male and female he created them" (NRSV Gen. 1:26-27). From the very beginning, there is no question of superiority or

4. See Timothy George's discussion of this theme in *Theology of the Reformers* (Nashville: Broadman Press, 1988), 59.

5. See John Leith's discussion of Calvin's doctrine of *sola gloria* in *John Calvin's Doctrine of the Christian Life* (Louisville: Westminster/John Knox Press, 1989), 37-45.

inferiority, between the sexes. Both are created with an equal capacity for self-transcendence and accountability, for intimate relationships and moral commitments. This essential uniqueness transcends either gender's sexuality or psycho-physical structure.

Furthermore, from a Christian perspective, in a manner similar to which God enjoys harmonious reciprocity within the mystery of the Trinity as God the Creator, God the Redeemer, and God the Holy Spirit, so, in the Genesis story, God wills that human beings experience as much reciprocity with the Divine and one another as human nature allows. To realize this potential, intelligence, moral interrelationships, and intimate personal commitments are required, which in turn make possible the ultimate sanctity of the marriage bond. In fact, this capacity for "reciprocity" signals the important role that, in the Hebrew Bible, family, personal relationships, covenants, and the basic institutions of society play in molding moral character.

According to the Yahwist account, God gave the archetypal couple not merely gifts of rationality and heightened moral sensibilities but *each other* ("It is not good that the man should be alone; I will make a helper fit for him." Gen. 2:18). In the Hebrew Bible, the intimacy of marriage, the network of the home, and the larger community of Israel are indispensable nurturing and fostering agents for the undergirding of the moral life. Both male and female need this nurturing. Both are members of a larger community, a multi-tiered network of personal relationships, that sustains them. The moral men and women of the Hebrew Bible are *interdependent* in a way that Aristotle's virtuous person is an individualist. Granted, male and female sexual experiences are different, the focal point of each gender's humanness transcends this sexual difference, to be grasped and molded by God and to be shared in community and intimacy with others. Our equality as creatures in the "image of God" supercedes our mere sexuality.

The third theme emerges from the metaphors of "dust" and "rib." However high and nobly gifted human beings may be, male and females are still finite. Human beings are limited by time and space and by all the natural, biological, and historical contingencies of existence. As such, they are sexually different, while both belonging together to nature and nature's orders and cycles.

Though biologically different in gender and structure, men and women are both finite, contingent, mortal creatures. Neither child of God can deny his or her gender or creatureliness without belying the truth about themselves. This is true of both genders, corporately and individually. Biblical men and women are contingent beings, each sex owing its existence to Another, whether created from "dust" or "rib." To deny their contingency, or to fail to appreciate each other's gender difference, or to aspire to a transcendence and status of independence that ignores their finitude, or to lapse into a passive despair because of it, is to destroy the bonds of mutuality that make them human. The stories depicting Cain's murder of Abel, the Noachean era's indifference to morals, and the desire of the builders of Babel to "make a name" for themselves all witness to this truth. There can be no genuine development of character, no sound growth in personhood and intimacy, where human creatureliness is spurned and men and women determine to become sovereign individuals (or dispairers of selfhood), independent of God or indifferent to each other's nature.

This coincides with Calvin's own understanding of humanness, in so far as he underscores the human need to glorify God (that is, to have a focal point for authenticity), by reminding his readers that they are not their own but belong to another. As he wrote to Cardinal Sadolet:

> It is not very sound theology to confine a man's thought so much to himself, and not to set before him, as the prime motive for his existence, zeal to illustrate the glory of God. For we are born first of all for God, and not for ourselves.[6]

The "dust" and "rib" motifs symbolize our belonging to God. In doing so, they confront believers, male and female, not merely with judgment, but with grace, since they remind all of the true foundation of human wholeness, which is inseparable from the mutual good of all.

Finally, the fourth theme has to do with the ultimate criterion of good. "You may freely eat of every tree of the garden; but of

6. Quoted by Leith, ibid., 37.

the tree of the knowledge of good and evil you shall not eat, for in the day that you eat of it you shall die" (Gen. 2:16-17). Who, in the final analysis, defines good? The Torah answers, simply and unequivocally, GOD. God — alone the giver of human dignity and determiner of human boundaries — is the highest determiner of "good" and "evil." This does not mean that human beings are not qualified to make distinctions between good and evil. Such a contention would be a denial of our creation in the "image of God." Rather, all human determinations of good and evil are to be measured against the divine will. When human beings determine good and evil aside from God's will, they do so in terms of their own best interests, race, gender, nation, or socio-economic class. But God defines "good" and "evil" in terms of humankind's highest good, for both genders as for all nations and peoples.

This is the foundation for understanding biblical virtue and its character-molding power.

The Patriarchal Narratives

Before examining the patriarchal sagas, their theological basis first needs to be highlighted. In the Hebrew Bible, the ancient patriarchal sagas stand as testimonies to God's free, electing initiative, by means of which God solicits faith in the Eternal's interaction with humankind, especially with the community of Israel. It is this theology that the narrator of the Old Epic sagas emphasizes. As such the sagas bear witness to God's choice of Israel and, in turn, are meant to reinforce Israel's own appreciation of God's election of the community. That God comes at all is a mystery that the sagas emphasize. It is God's coming, the Eternal's decision to come to God's creatures and from among them elect a specific family through which to bless all the families of the earth that is, for Judaism, the occasion for awakening in the people of God the possibility of their becoming truly human.

Abraham and Sarah

The narratives begin with Abraham and Sarah. It begins with both of them, because they are a unit, a single fabric of humanity in relationship. Abraham would not be Abraham without Sarah, nor she Sarah without him. Even when the Hebrew Bible speaks only of him, she is near at hand.

The Judeo-Christian tradition has always extolled Abraham for his *faith*. He is the "knight of faith," to borrow Kierkegaard's phrase,[7] or, to borrow Luther's, the "exemplar" par excellence. This is Judaism's view as well, for it is his example of faith that the Genesis story exalts. "And he believed the Lord; and he reckoned it to him as righteousness" (Gen. 15:6). The Hebrew word for "believe" is *'aman*. In its finest sense, it means to be *firm*, fixed in one's intention and resolution, *stable*, sure about one's response. It implies a high and demanding virtue, and it is a mistake to suppose there is in it anything facile or sentimental. But if faith is Abraham's central virtue, it is a multi-dimensional virtue and one which invites further investigation.

As for Sarah, it is her sensitivity and pride, her realism and awareness of her closeness to Nature ("After I have grown old, . . . shall I have pleasure?" NRSV Gen. 18:12), that, in both the traditional and feminist views, have either marred or commended her as an exemplar. Certainly, in Genesis, the Old Epic account of Sarah preserves her humanness to a fault, and no simple virtues can be isolated from the overall context of her barrenness and jealously, and later, from her fecundity and joy.

The gravest danger one can do, however, to either Abraham or Sarah, is to idolize him at her expense. Not even the Bible does this, though it does portray him as the unique champion of faith, alone and single of his kind, an exemplar for human meditation as long as humanity endures. But Abraham and Sarah are equally human and readers can identify with both of them, but especially with Sarah and her need to laugh at the thought of becoming pregnant at ninety in order to survive the cruelties of her barren-

7. See Kierkegaard's *Fear and Trembling*, trans. Walter Lowrie (Garden City: Anchor Books, 1941), 27-64.

ness. Indeed, even Sarah's ability to laugh will become a virtue in time. But the events that engulf them are of God's doing. As a result, their lives cease to be their own; they fully belong to God, in spite of all their insecurities, ambiguities, and anguish, of which they have plenty. They are not spared any of life's tension. And Abraham's faith, if perfected at all, is done so only in the coals of a searing and demanding realism, while Sarah's "feminine experience" is given new focus and transcendence.

Of the many things that might be said of Abraham and Sarah's faith, three nuances of faith are clearly discernable in the tradition that has preserved their saga. (1) Faith is a positive response to the Eternal God, who, in the mystery of grace, encounters humankind on God's terms, not humankind's. (2) It is the confident belief that this God alone is the One whose care for humanity cannot be superseded. (3) Faith, in time, accepts the Eternal's ordering will for the universe as life's highest good. This multidimensional faith enhances moral character.

First, both Abraham and Sarah do respond, by grace, to the Eternal God, who, in the profundity of the divine revelation, confronts them as the undeniable reality with whom they have to do. God alone emerges as the unquestioned focal point of existence for both of them. Beyond every sound and ethical rule that human beings unaided are capable of discerning, Abraham is drawn, by the living God, to rise above the ethos of his Amorite-Sumerian culture and to open his life to the God of the universe itself. So too is Sarah. "God has brought laughter for me; everyone who hears will laugh with me" (NRSV Gen. 21:6). From the standpoint of the Hebrew meaning of faith, here is that *stability* that humankind is invited to seek and find only in the Eternal.

Pursuing this a step further, whatever Abraham's duties in Haran were, however extensive his ethical obligations to his father's family that had migrated there from Ur, by God's grace, the patriarch's conscience is required to acknowledge a dimension of life larger than any commitment he owed to his culture's ethical principles. Hence, again, the saga witnesses to that *stability*, that *foundation*, that anchors and fixes one's entire life, but it is a foundation made possible only because of God's initiative.

"Now the Lord said to Abram, 'Go from your country and

your kindred and your father's house to the land that I will show you'" (Gen. 12:1). And so Abraham goes in obedience to the Eternal, bearing witness to that reality which alone can stabilize and satisfy his life. And in doing so, he becomes painfully aware that the purpose of human creation is not merely to serve the ethical spheres of one's time, but to know and to serve God, who alone can lift life to its highest joy. So also Sarah, who moves beyond the grudging ethics of sharing her handmaid, Hagar, with her husband, to the joy of fulfillment in childbearing.

In the philosophical sense, this nuance declares that faith is foundational and that its repercussions for moral development are immense.

Second, both Abraham and Sarah, as time evolves, become aware of the *de profundis* nature of God as love. Time is required to perceive this, as there are moments when each has doubts. Ultimately, however, both come to realize that the Eternal's relentless and remorseless demands spring from a foundation of love that issues in wholeness. This is the irony of God's command: "Take your son, your only son Isaac, whom you love, and go to the land of Moriah, and offer him there as a burnt offering . . ." (Gen. 22:2), which in great anguish Abraham prepares himself to do. So he goes to Moriah and lifts the knife, believing, that though he shall slay his and Sarah's son, yet God will give him back, because God has promised them an heir. No one can ignore the anguish or terror Abraham feels, or the risk he takes, as he raises that knife, that knife of faith that must rip through everything relative if believers are to know God. That is what makes biblical faith the highest kind of faith: the anguished risk that the God of Scripture who confronts one in the divine self-revelation is alone life's highest good and that at heart that good is the Infinite Love. And in turn it is the risk that God's goodness is what redeems life and fills each finite moment with stability, anchorage, purpose, and peace. True, one may not become "better," or even suffer less anxiety. But by grace such faith, as a foundational stabilizing response, deepens one's humanness and character.

Third, Abraham and Sarah alike come in time to accept God's providential ordering of life as containing life's highest good. The virtue of faith that this saga illustrates is characterized by the acceptance of what God wills as equivalent to what is best. It is what the Eternal orders or allows — however different from one's own agenda it might appear to be, or however impossible it might strike one from the viewpoint of life's cycles — that makes life's highest good possible. It is faith characterized by trust in God's ordering of life and not contingent on human demands. And it is this insight that brings perspective to, if not patience in, the tense and inscrutable moments of existence. In the Hebrew, the verb "provide" *(jireh)* expresses the depth of this possibility. "God will provide," said Abraham, as he ran his fingers tremblingly through the knotted hair of the child he loved. And because God provides, God can be trusted. One can fix and stabilize one's life on this God.

Faith is not the only virtue this story exalts. There are others, too, but they seem to flow from Abraham's trust in God and intense commitment to God's will, and from Sarah's discovery of what alone brings her fulfillment as a woman. That is the order the narrator seems to prefer. As a consequence, the couple's lives take on a mode of existence that allows other characteristics to surface and shape their destinies. In that light, a number of subordinate virtues comes into play. Among them are Abraham's *transcendence of the purely egoistic,* as well as his *transcendence of the purely materialistic.* We see this both in his attitude toward himself and in his largesse to his nephew and the religious institutions of his day (the gift to the priest at Salem). But this does not make him any less able a provider, for he had accumulated great wealth, which he enjoyed in all of its materialistic and pleasurable forms. The Hebrew Bible extols prosperity, because it has no misgivings about poverty: poverty enslaves, demeans, and can destroy lives. But prosperity provides the means needed for sustaining life and for opening life up to deeper possibilities. Though Abraham pursues wealth, it never becomes an end in itself. Rather, it is a good he enjoys and uses to higher ends: to share with his kindred and with the servants of God.

As for Sarah, it is the *intensity of her realism* and the *depth of her inner personhood* that the story emphasizes, which enable her to bear her role as a woman, wed to Abraham. It is she who endures the potential abuse of Abraham's suggestion to Pharaoh and who suffers Abraham's deference to Lot and preference for a nomadic existence. And it is Sarah who exercises the initiative by suggesting that Abraham take Hagar and, by this servant girl, father children for both their good, if not God's. In all of this she displays *strength* and *depth* of character, not perversity or passivity. Indeed, her *initiative* witnesses to her own conviction that her personal fate and destiny are both hers to suffer, as well as to account for and entrust to God.

As for Abraham, the saga depicts the patriarch as a man of *kindness* and *tolerance* toward all whose claims against him are ethically just. This is especially true of those whom he has wronged. Here, the story points to Hagar and Ishmael's lawful claims upon Abraham's love, protection, and property, which he satisfies because, by moral law, it is his duty to do so. But, though he loves them, he turns away because of God's greater claim on his life. The Eternal's love embraces Hagar and Ishmael throughout their ordeal and out of compassion, establishes her and her son's future. But Abraham could have driven them off and out of his life without the first sign of pity, or, cursing the day he succumbed to Sarah's advice, he might, with an intolerable sense of guilt and resentment, have done violence to Hagar and her child. However, he did not, because he loved them and recognized his duty toward them. He will not blame them for his ambivalence, but without resentment or spite shows them kindness and tolerance. His actions remind one of Unamuno's dictum: "The good man is not good because he believes in a transcendental order, but rather he believes in it because he is good."[8] Yet, whence this human "good"? The Hebrew Bible traces it to God and God's secret interplay with the human heart.

Finally, there is both Abraham and Sarah's *acceptance* of the inscrutable exigencies of life. We watch this acceptance grace their lives with dignity as they wander through the land that God has promised them and as they part company with Lot, to face an unknown tomorrow. We watch it especially grace the old patriarch's later years as he barters with sadness, yet with Bedouin

8. Miguel de Unamuno, *Essays & Soliloquies*, trans. J. E. Crawford Flitch (New York: Alfred A. Knopf, 1925), 155.

pride, for Sarah's grave, where, beside her, he knows that he himself will lie in time.

But these are secondary virtues; by observing them Abraham did not become the "knight of faith" nor Sarah the woman of new-found joy and transcendent focus. On the contrary, these characteristics become part of them and deepen their experience as children of God and father and mother of a nation, because when God sought them, they responded to the Eternal with a Yes. Or, in Sarah's case, with *awe,* as she holds her son to her breasts and says, "Who would have ever said to Abraham that Sarah would nurse children?" (NRSV Gen. 21:7).

In the light of this narrative, we are required not to idolize either Abraham or Sarah. Rather, we are challenged to internalize a *trusting acceptance of God* as providing life's highest hope, which alone is able to encourage, fulfill, and deepen our human-ness and self-actualization. That is what the virtue of faith is about and why it is so important in the biblical record and to a biblical ethic. God's children live for more than fulfilling the moral law or the requirements of our sexual nature. We were created for God, for the glory of God, which alone stabilizes human action and dispositions. And such faith comes to believers only as it came to Abraham and Sarah, as one commits oneself to God in the midst of one's own anxieties, tensions, and inse-curities. That is what makes biblical faith the higher kind of faith and what deepens one's humanity as a person and as a moral agent.

Jacob

If faith is the virtue extolled in the Abraham-Sarah saga, what is the virtue par excellence of the Jacob story? In a phrase, it is the community of Israel's *awareness of God's faithfulness* in God's "everlasting covenant," or, in Hebrew, the *berith olam.* It takes Jacob, himself, a lifetime to realize this, but once he discovers it, it deepens his wholeness as a human being.

Cherishing an awareness of the faithfulness of God, however late it may come, is an authentic virtue, exemplified in the Jacob saga. In the Hebrew Bible, God's "everlasting covenant" and the *hesed* love of God's steadfast loyalty constitute the community's first and foremost presupposition. Thus, calling to memory God's faithfulness, God's promises to the patriarchs, and, later, reciting the great *Heilsgeschichte* moments of God's activity in Israel's behalf, deepens one's sense of existence, with all its possibilities for fellowship and reciprocity with God and neighbor.

This patriarchal story also reminds readers that, time and again, human strength fails, but not God's. God's faithfulness in the midst of human faithlessness has the power to renew human life. In essence, that is the meaning of Jacob's dream at Bethel (Gen. 28) and possibly a central reason why the stories about him were both created and preserved. Whenever the community of Israel called to mind God's faithfulness to Jacob, it served to lift them up, especially when their own virtuous activities were, at best, questionable.

As in the case with Abraham, however, the believer must guard against being too self-assured, lest one minimize one's own personal potential for evil or overlook one's neighbor's for good. Jacob seems constantly to have underestimated his own potential for evil and mistrusted his neighbor's potential for good. From the time he is old enough to perceive that Esau is his father's favorite, a cunning determination to best both his brother and his enemies becomes one of Jacob's defining characteristics. He never loses it; not even in the end, when as an old man he rebukes Joseph for his dreams: "Shall I and your mother . . . come to bow ourselves to the ground before you?" (Gen. 37:10). Here is a pride that remains intact to the very end.

Yet the Genesis Torah neither asks believers to pity Jacob nor to condemn him. This story is careful to do neither. Rather he serves as a mirror for Israel — who bears his name (Gen. 32:32), and a mirror, if not for all humankind, at least for the "masculine experience."

From the moment Jacob determines to supplant his brother, a different hero of the sojourn emerges. On the one hand, he is crafty, industrious, extremely independent, and a survivor. Yet, on the other, Jacob is Israel's true prince of the patriarchs, perhaps even more so than Abraham. For this all-too-human grandson of the great "knight of faith" is nonetheless haunted by the Eternal, though his soul yearns for ends other than God's. This is his irony as well as the story's. He can be such an unfaithful sovereign individual, yet his very qualities of *ambition, resolve,* and *tenacity* are virtues of no mean significance for service in the kingdom of God. That Jacob often misuses them does not militate against their worth or devalue them as gifts useful to God. However ruthless and uncaring regarding his brother's stature by his father's doting love and preference for Esau, the believing community can readily see that God's purposes for Isaac's posterity far transcend Esau's preference for lentils, or Isaac's fondness for the smell of hides and fields. Jacob had to leave home. He is a prototype of the Prodigal Son. And it is to Rebekah's glory, to his mother's insight, that she concurs and encourages him to do so. The Hebrew Bible faults neither her nor him for their *courage* or *wisdom* in this matter. Rebekah's own *ambition, resolve,* and *tenacity* turn out to be theologically sound. If anything, the story applauds Rebekah for her actions and instincts, as they are both subordinate and committed to the will of God.

That Jacob continues to deal shrewdly with everyone in his path, and prospering in the process, is amply testified to in the remaining story. It affirms the biblical conviction, which is silently brought out in the longer story, that there are qualities of attitude and action, of *determination* and *resoluteness,* that a "hero of the sojourn" must internalize and exercise if he or she is to survive in the world of one's neighbor as well as be of service to God. Had Jacob remained subservient or submissive to his father-in-law in the land of Aram and remained there till death, would not God, according to this story, have been forced to find another Abraham, another Sarah, another "hero of the sojourn" with courage to risk a Yes in the divine call — however conniving he or she might have been at times?

The Bible even says of Jacob: "Your name shall no more be called Jacob, but Israel, for you have striven with God and with men, and have prevailed" (Gen. 32:28). He was a contender, a contender with GOD and neighbor. And he prevailed! "I will not let you go," he says to God, "unless you bless me" (Gen. 32:26).

Again, we are not meant to pity or to condemn this "hero of

the sojourn." Nor should we take his contentious spirit out of context, demean him or his mother for their tenacity, ambition, and resolve, nor judge him for his mettle and self-assurance. Nonetheless, it was not by exercising these "virtues" that Jacob became the kind of latter-day "knight of faith" he is, prevailing with God and men. Rather, because God refused to abandon the Divine promises to Abraham, and because God remained faithful to Jacob wherever the latter sojourned, Jacob came to realize that his life, contrary to his own bent and achievements, belonged not to himself but to the Eternal; that his life all along had been a life lived "in the presence of God." And so he limps across the Jabbok Brook, broken in pride, but ennobled because now his life has been deepened by God, his humanness thoroughly sounded, and his mind and heart claimed by and for the Eternal.

Joseph

If Abraham is the "knight of faith" par excellence, and Jacob the maverick "hero of the sojourn," Joseph's life is even more symbolic and his virtues equally paradigmatic for the believing community. In Joseph the Hebrew Bible confronts us with the "saintly sage," the consummate wise servant of Israel's faith, whose heart, mind, and strength are totally committed to God and neighbor. Tradition has so polished him that his virtues are highly unattainable, almost transcendent, so that he emerges as the biblical man of virtue without equal, with, perhaps, the exception of Job.

Yet this saga portrays Joseph equally as a true *human*, whose life, in spite of the romantic and nationalistic elements that now appear to be associated with it, was subject to as many insecurities and tensions as was Abraham's and Sarah's. Son of his father's favorite bride and son of Jacob's old age, there appears never to be a conscious moment when Joseph is not aware of his brothers' jealousy and resentment. The writer says they "hated him" and treated him with contempt: "they . . . could not speak peaceably to him" (Gen. 37:4). Still he bears their hate and his own father's rebuke (Gen. 37:10) with *equanimity*. Indeed, this quality of *equanimity* characterizes his entire life and sets him apart from the other principals of the story. So the question the text raises is: whence this *equanimity* that sets him apart and molds his life and character? It is, of course, a quality that members of the believing community can also have. But first we should understand its source.

In the narrative, its source is the mystery of God, the Eternal, whose electing initiative rests upon Joseph and claims him and his life. The storyteller delays full disclosure of this theme until the end of the saga. But, once again, it is God who acts first, who sets the stage for the human response. At the outset, the lad is seventeen, yet his subconscious is preoccupied with stirrings that cause him to wonder. Even his dream-life is pervaded by the Eternal, though he is too young to draw the requisite theological inferences. Still, the experience fills him with a strange *equanimity;* for in spite of his brothers' "hate," he continues to share his dreams with them. Though he cannot render his feelings into an adequate theological insight, he is already cognizant of the truth that, from a perspective of God's ordering will for the universe, neither "hate" nor "contempt" must be allowed to have the last word. From his youth, he perceives what took his great-grandfather, Abraham, a lifetime to articulate: that a *trust in God's providential ordering of life leads to life's highest good.* What Abraham mumbled on the way to Moriah ("God will provide") Joseph acknowledges in his dreams. For Joseph knows that something profound is astir and that its essence is the *euangelion,* the good news that God can be trusted, that God is at work in the universe for good, however jealous, hateful, and contemptuous "brothers" may be. As he would say to them years later: "You meant evil against me; but God meant it for good" (Gen. 50:20). For "God sent me before you to *preserve life.* . . . God sent me . . . to *preserve* for you a remnant on earth, and *to keep alive* for you many survivors. So it was not you . . . but God" (NRSV Gen. 45:5, 7-8). The Hebrew verb *hajah,* which means "to save," "save alive" to "guard" or "preserve," here translated "to preserve life" and "to keep alive" is operative here. It is because God does this *preserving, saving alive, guarding of life,* and the *sending* of servants to fulfill the divine purposes, that the Israelite community can dare to attend to its own and life's larger, moral and ethical concerns.

For the narrator, it is this kind of faith in God's preserving activity and goodness that can sustain Israel. For the narrator, it is this faith that produces Joseph's *equanimity* which, in the face of hate, abuse, assault, and slavery, sustains him until he is brought to Potiphar's house and, in time, to pharaoh's attention. It is this faith, with its trust in God's ordering goodness, that also frees him to devote his God-given intellectual and moral capacities to serve, first his master Potiphar with loyalty and faithfulness, and then his state and the common good with the physical and mental strength required to plan for and manage the state in a seven-year famine.

From the narrator's perspective, this equanimity can belong to Israel and all members of the believing community, wherever they are gathered. But the point of this saga, in particular, is that such equanimity flows from a trust in God's providential ordering. This equanimity can be practiced by both male and female. Our world is no different from Joseph's; hate and jealousy still reign and work their enslaving powers. Trust in God's ordering goodness and divine call can lift life above such hate. It can free one from the tentacles of spite and gossip in order to use one's intellectual and moral capacities, emotional and relational gifts, for the glory of God and love of neighbor.

The Pentateuchal Legal Heritage

As a genre, the legal sections of the Pentateuch are set within a theological narrative that provides an essential prologue for the Covenant and its stipulations. Out of the theology embedded in this prologue, Israel's ethical commitments procede. This prologue (Exod. 19:1–20:2) includes three central ideas.

The first is the significant role the narrator assigns to the *theophany* of God at Sinai. What this narrative champions is the glory of God, the awesome, splendor of the Divine One. The starting point for all biblical ethics is always the holiness, grace, and majesty of God. This is what the *theophany* celebrates. It is not the human capacity to serve high moral ends that is exalted in the Hebrew Bible. Rather, the focus is rightfully upon God and what God wills and accomplishes for humankind.

The second is the Hebrew command to "obey" God's voice and to "keep" God's commandments. The Hebrew verb for both words is *sama'*, which means to both *hear* and *obey*, to take to heart what God has told you and to *do* it. It is not too radical to claim that all Old Testament ethics is rooted in this *theophanous* event at Sinai, for which *obedience* to God is the only sane and proper human response. In the light of who God is and what God does, heeding God's voice by keeping and loving God's will is the only appropriate human reaction that can generate stability and sanity. Such "keeping" requires steadfast commitment, vigilance, renewal, the investment of the self over and over again in the only thing that matters most — the voice, will, and grace of God.

Third is the idea of being God's "treasured possession" (NRSV Exod. 19:5). Moses would have approved of Calvin's "we are not our own . . ." theology. The whole idea of election, of being treasured and loved by the God of theophanous glory, provides the theological context for both the Decalogue and the Covenant Code's "virtues."

Once again, the Hebrew Bible invites readers to acknowledge first things first. These sections are expressive of God's love, which comes first. These documents exist, are given only because of God, and, although they reflect the narrator's time, culture, and his understanding of the moral law, they finally express the *hesed* will of God. About them, even Jesus said, "I have not come to abolish the law and the prophets but to fulfill them" (Matt. 5:17). The believing community is asked to remember as well the communal nature of these laws, their covenantal context, that they were given to and cherished by the people of Israel — who loved and taught them and sought to embody them as a people, unique to God.

Of the many facets of the legal tradition that could be examined, four merit special attention: (1) the Decalogue, (2) the Covenant Code, (3) the Holiness Code, and (4) the Deuteronomic Torah.

The Decalogue

It begins with grace and concludes in awe. These two aspects of the Divine theophany, of the Divine encounter, are difficult to separate. The grace of God is awesome to experience, and the awe that God elicits is aroused by divine grace. "I am the Lord your God, who brought you out of the land of Egypt, out of the house of bondage" (Exod. 20:2). Here are both grace and awe. "Do not fear; for God has come to prove you, . . . that the fear of him may be before your eyes, that you may not sin" (Exod. 20:20). Calvin would refer to the phenomenon as "the majesty of God," or "the honor of God," which is his way of acknowledging this theophanous element.

> Hence that dread and wonder with which Scripture commonly represents the saints as stricken and overcome whenever they felt the presence of God. . . . As a consequence, we must infer that man is never sufficiently touched and affected by the awareness of his lowly state until he has compared himself with God's majesty. (*Inst.* 1.1.3)

Awe and grace. Grace and Awe. These are the twin *sine qua nons* of the Decalogue, of the entire Mosaic Torah, that frame the boundaries within which the Law's "virtues" and its importance for moral character becomes tenable.

The First Table of the Law (Exod. 20:3-11)

As Walther Eichrodt explains: "The really remarkable feature of the Decalogue is . . . *the definite connection of the moral precepts with the basic religious commands.* It is the expression of a conviction that moral action is inseparably bound up with the worship of God."[9] From that perspective, the first four commandments have to do clearly with "the honor of God." They teach believers that to honor God, or to love God, is a dispositional virtue of singular magnitude. Where the *honor of God* is practiced and

9. Walther Eichrodt, *The Theology of the Old Testament,* trans. J. A. Baker (Philadelphia: Westminster Press, 1961), I, 76.

pursued, the deepening of one's humanness and moral resolve will follow. Where God is the highest of all loyalties ("no other gods"), esteemed above every temptation to enrobe God in finite form — however aesthetic ("no graven images"), respected above every attempt to trivialize or empty the Eternal of divine power ("The sacredness of the Name"), and when human finitude and temporaneity are continually revitalized by the infinity and timelessness of God ("Remember the Sabbath day"), then a true foundation is laid for one's development as God's partner, created in the divine image with genuine potential for growth and good. Thus *to practice the honor of God* is the first virtue that the Decalogue extols.

The Second Table of the Law (Exod. 20:12-17)

Growing out of this consciousness of God, a host of subsequent virtues emerge. They are universal ethical virtues, which are therefore relational and communal and known by all civilized peoples. Aristotle would have recognized them as virtues. They form that part of the Eternal will which God is pleased for the rational to know and by means of which God blesses the families of the earth. Or in Aquinas's mind, they constitute those virtues which allow all humanity to experience a happy, though "imperfect," life now. They enable all human beings to enjoy a sense of satisfaction — however limited.

A careful reading of the Second Table reveals at least *five* virtues that are ethical and universal and which belong to the sphere of the relational. They are *gratitude, respect, faithfulness* (fidelity), *truthfulness,* and *contentment.* These are the virtues behind, pervading, and undergirding the Second Table of the law, adherence to which results in a *stable* and *sane* ordering for all — males and females. Certainly the community of Israel cherished them to this end. They have to do with the *honoring of human life.* They are cherished by God, though, in Western philosophy, one can know them without knowing God. But from both a biblical and a Christian perspective, this is acceptable, since God loves all men and women even when they do not know or love God. In spite of this, God always wills the best for them. Hence this ordering need not be questioned, because it serves for every human being's good and provides for a level of reciprocity among all humankind, even in an imperfect world. Here again the believer stands in the shadow of grace and awe, in the shadow of God's *theophany.*

Whenever humans treat each other with *gratitude* (the Fifth Commandment) and *respect* (the Fifth through the Ninth Commandments), in *faithfulness* and *truthfulness* (Commandments Seven and Eight), without envy and spite (Commandments Six, Eight, and Ten), then human beings are truly free to use their God-given potential for intellectual and moral good in a way that sustains society as well as fulfills one's personal good. These virtues are universal humanizing qualities and mirror God's will for all. No one should be surprised to discover that they are extolled not only by ancient societies but also by contemporary Hindus, Buddhists, and Moslems. According to the Judeo-Christian tradition, they are derived from the only divine, holy, and eternal power there is: GOD, Creator of all.

The Covenant Code

Immediately following the Decalogue, the book of Exodus contains, what scholars call the Covenant Code. It is found in Exodus 20:22–23:33. It reflects a period sometime after the Israelite conquest of Canaan and represents Israel's effort, as a community, to govern itself in the light of God's covenant made at Sinai and later renewed at Shechem.

Like the Decalogue, its laws also reflect the phenomenon of the universal ethical, for they include virtues knowable to reason and rational contemplation. But, at the same time, the laws fall also under the influence of the *theophanous* encounter, with its emphasis on *"heeding"* and *"obedience."* Accordingly, the laws, here, are molded by Israel's special knowledge of the Eternal, that similar codes of the time, such as the Code of Hammurabi, could not reflect. According to Eichrodt, three factors contribute to the Covenant Code's distinctive difference from the Code of Hammurabi. First, it places a "higher value . . . on human life"; second, it abolishes "gross brutality in the punishment of the guilty"; and, third, it rejects "any class-distinction in the administration of justice."[10] What, then, are the virtues of this Covenant Code and are they still relevant for the believing community?

Though the virtues of the Covenant Code remain, broadly speaking, relevant, it is less easy to discern what they are. In general it may be assayed that the five virtues of the Second Table appear also in the Code. However, they are applied to specific human conditions pertinent to the Israelite community at the time. The Code is divided into three main sections.

Section I (Exod. 21:1-32) is devoted to laws protecting human beings. Granted, the feminists are right to remind modern readers that the society that created this Code was "male-dominated," "hierarchical," and "authoritarian." Nonetheless, at the heart of these laws stands the principle of *honoring human life,* which is not "gender-specific." No matter how lowly (from the household slave to the daughter sold into slavery) or how highly esteemed (a property owner whose ox inadvertently gores a human being), principles of *respect, gratitude, faithfulness,* and *truthfulness* are to be applied however the patriarchal society of Israel might have abused them. Only then is a just society achieved, or each human being freed to exercise his or her intellectual and moral capacities to the fullest. In this context, even the law of equivalent retaliation — the *lex talionis* — is given a universal and humane setting, for the victims of crime, as well as their families, may exact no more from the perpetrators than a fair equivalent — "life for life, eye for eye, tooth for tooth" (Exod. 21:23-24). A respect for human life, created in the image of God, protects the offender as well as the victim and, just as importantly, functions to keep each person human and humane. Does not even Jesus say: "Love your enemies . . . so that you may be sons of your Father who . . . makes his sun rise on the evil and on the good, and sends rain on the just and on the unjust" (Matt. 5:44-45)? The honoring of human life is central.

Section II (Exod. 21:33–22:17) focuses on property disputes and equitable ways of resolving them. In each case, *truthfulness, faithfulness,* and *respect* are critical — again, however limited they

10. Ibid., 77-79.

might have been applied at the time. Adherence to these principles establishes dispositions and actions that mold character and contribute to the common good. They deepen humanity and strengthen the human capacity for lasting and rewarding partnerships of reciprocity and fellowship.

Of particular interest in this section is the Israelite commitment to the principle of *restitution*. Determining the appropriate sum one should pay an individual who has been wronged has never been easy. Aristotle devotes a chapter to this identical problem in his *Nicomachean Ethics* and, if he falls short of solving it, at least addresses the questions of hurt, loss, and fairness that sufferers of wrong desire to see redressed. Aristotle concludes that "restitution" is a form of justice and without "restitution," or its counterpart, commitments to justice are empty. The same appears to be true in the Covenant Code.

Restitution as a form of *justice* sharpens one's understanding of justice as a virtue. It forces individuals to ask: "What do I owe my fellow human being? What specific attitudes and acts help me *honor* my neighbor, so that I do not deprive my neighbor of all that constitutes his or her true humanness?" As such, this Hebrew principle of restitution represents not simply an *a posteriori* virtue, or one to be exercised after the fact, but a preventive one, one to be exercised *a priori*, in advance, of all one's relationships with one's neighbors. Is it not included in Jesus' own saying, in which he endorses the same preventive measure: "Do unto others as you would have them do unto you" (KJV Matt. 7:12)? That is applying justice before the fact, because it is what humans owe each other as persons created in the image of God, endowed with high potential for individual development in reciprocity with each other.

The *last section* of the Covenant Code (Exod. 22:18–23:9) seeks to address a number of social and cultic issues. Again, the central virtue is justice. But this time justice is defined in terms of *compassion*. It is delineated in terms of a positive outreach for all genders and classes caught short-handed in society's social and economic structures.

In particular the stranger, the widow, the orphan, and the poor are called to the community's attention. "You shall not wrong a stranger or oppress him. . . . You shall not afflict any widow or orphan. . . . You shall not exact interest from [the poor]" (Exod. 22:21-25). Why? Not simply because the Israelites were once themselves strangers. But because the Creator and Redeemer God of Israel is merciful. "I am compassionate" (Exod. 22:27).

The Code's theme of compassion is especially welcomed by the feminist movement. Riane Eisler, in particular, argues that themes of compassion, caring, and nurture were, from the earliest periods of Sumerian culture, recognized as "feminine" values.[11] Harvard educational psychologist Carol Gilligan also emphasizes the value of an "ethics of care" versus an "ethics of justice," particularly for women. Writes Gilligan:

> Since the reality of interconnexion is experienced by women as given rather than freely contracted, they arrive at an understanding of life that reflects the limits of autonomy and control. . . . [They] perceive and construe social reality differently from men . . . because women's sense of integrity appears to be intertwined with an ethics of care.[12]

As for the Code, its implied principle is quite clear. There can be no well-ordering of humankind where one's neighbor (child or female, rich or poor) is overlooked. No adherence to the First Table of the Law can substitute for the dismissal of the Second. Any honoring of God that ignores human need is self-contradictory and morally inadequate. As T. B. Maston puts it: "There are no duties to God that relieve man of his duties to his neighbor."[13] What the Code champions is a universal principle, which is hardly the peculiar possession of Christianity or Judaism alone. Even the current Dalai Lama of Tibetan Buddhism has said: "My true religion is kindness."[14]

In the view of this Code, one cannot fulfill one's humanness aside from a positive outreach, expressed in the form of *compas-*

11. Riane Eisler, *The Chalice and the Blade* (San Francisco: HarperSan-Francisco, 1987), 85.

12. Carol Gilligan, *In A Different Voice* (Cambridge: Harvard Press, 1982), 171-72.

13. T. B. Maston, *Biblical Ethics: A Guide to the Ethical Message of the Scriptures from Genesis through Revelation* (Mercer University Press, 1982), 18.

14. *Time,* April 11, 1988, 60.

sion for every human being. If believers are not personally involved in some form of compassionate outreach — however limited — then they are deluding themselves.

The God who made humanity in the divine image is compassionate; therefore, that God should long for the human community also to be compassionate is hardly a mystery. It is part of God's hope for everyone, that as each person grows in grace and compassion, he or she will become an embodiment of divine mercy. Thus, as believers begin to actualize their high potential, by expressing compassion, and begin to redress the many forms of human need around them, they will experience that moral wholeness God longs for them to know.

"It is not good that the man should be alone," says God (Gen. 2:18). Humans require each other; a person cannot be human without another; individuals were not meant to go it alone. Each must care for the other, especially for the most "lonely" and "neglected": the stranger, the widow, the orphan, and the poor.

In the final analysis, what the Covenant Code embraces is an "ethics of compassion." One might even argue that it subsumes the universal, traditionalist "ethics of justice" within that "ethics of caring" that feminists espouse. It does so because God, in fullness of the Divine mystery, transcends the abstract and rational, and undergirds it with feeling, intimacy, and embracement — what some, indeed, have called the "feminine virtues."

The Holiness Code

In addition to the Covenant Code, the Pentateuch also preserves a section of Torahic tradition known as the Holiness Code. It is found in Leviticus 17–26 and contains a large corpus of laws characterized by their emphasis on "the holiness of God" — since God is holy, Israel, the community itself, is to be holy.

Upon first reading, these laws appear to be highly antiquated and outmoded, though possessing a strange appeal. One can understand why Calvin would succumb to the power of their logic and create a false theocracy based, not on grace, but on distinctions between "clean" and "unclean" rather than on love of God and

love of neighbor. Calvin would infer from these passages that no
one may marry a deceased spouse's sister or brother without violating the sanctity of God's true ordering of human life.

However, upon closer examination, the principles of *honoring
God* and *honoring neighbor* once again prove to be the crucial
determinants, but with a variance that makes them unique — the
holiness motif. In Hebrew, the word for "holy" is *qados*. It means
"to be different" or to be "separated" and suggests both a separation unto God and a separation from the world.[15] As a motif,
holiness means that the community of Israel is to be different
because God is different. It is this motif, with its emphasis on the
uniqueness of God, that is the central factor here. It is a virtue
that is significant for its character-molding power, because it has
the capacity to deepen and illumine one's true self-understanding
as a moral agent. Because the Creator-God, the Eternal Lord of
time and history, is unlike all else in time and history, what makes
human beings unique emanates from God. When it is drawn from
any other principle, or cause, or any other factor, the moral life
and reciprocity are spiritually obstructed from attaining their goal.
In accordance with this insight, whenever human life is content to
rise no higher than the natural, or, even worse, content to settle
for an ethics as "leveling" as Canaanism, then human uniqueness
and reciprocity are lost, at least as God meant them to function.
The Code makes this very clear:

> And the Lord said to Moses, "Say to the people of Israel, I
> am the Lord your God. You shall not do as they do in the land
> of Egypt, where you dwelt, and you shall not do as they do in
> the land of Canaan, to which I am bringing you. You shall not
> walk in their statutes. You shall do my ordinances and keep my
> statutes and walk in them. I am the Lord your God. You shall
> therefore keep my statutes and my ordinances, by doing which
> a man shall live: I am the Lord." (Lev. 18:5)

> And the Lord said to Moses, "Say to all the congregation of
> the people of Israel, You shall be holy; for I the Lord your God
> am holy." (Lev. 19:2)

15. Maston, *Biblical Ethics,* 23-24.

Notice that the Hebrew emphasis here falls on the verb to *keep (samar)*. It is this concept of "keeping" the "statutes" and the "ordinances" of God that the Priestly writer underscores. This sense of "keeping" is critical, for, in Hebrew, the word at once implies *watching, guarding, protecting, preserving, retaining, observing,* and finally *doing,* the revealed will of God, manifest in the Torah. As in the case of "believing," "keeping" the Torah is no simple virtue, no simple demand on a moral agent. But it is the fitting response to God's redemptive activity bringing Israel out of Egypt. It mirrors God's highest hope for Israel, and is possible for them to adventure, because of God's steadfast loyalty (*hesed* love) to Abraham and God's commitment to the *berith olam*.

By way of inference, then, this call to separateness and difference, loyalty and commitment, requires *wisdom* and *courage*. Wisdom because it recognizes that, where humankind's highest good is concerned, God alone can be the final determiner of good and evil, not culture, nor technology, nor nature. Especially not the latter, as nature, too, is God's created order. And courage because to adhere to and "to keep" an ethic different from the value systems enjoined by one's political and national state requires fortitude, persistence, and determination. It is what Aristotle meant by "moral strength," which can only be generated by the exercise of courage and self-control. Thus the Code enjoins believers to actualize what they know to be true: that only an ethic of God first and neighbor on a par with oneself can overcome an ethic of selfishness, spite, or loss of self-awareness. Only when "clean" and "unclean" are defined in terms of love of God and love of neighbor is the foundation laid "by doing which a man shall live."

Thus the Holiness Code reminds the community of faith that wisely and courageously *keeping* God's revealed hope for humankind is what, in turn, keeps life human. When the grace of God and the love of God's will (again, as symbolized in the *keeping* of the Torah) are put first, then they undergird the virtues of *respect, truthfulness, gratitude,* and *faithfulness,* which lift life above the tragic unraveling that claims so much of human existence.

The Deuteronomic Torah

The central text of this corpus is Deuteronomy 7:6-11. In its pages we meet for the second time *(deutero)* those critical themes, with their implied virtues, which we have met earlier. Again, we meet the unique and sole Creator-God of the universe, whose free electing initiative comes first, and who, out of the mystery of the divine grace and love, creates the order by which the families of the earth are destined to be blessed. In this torah the Eternal spells out the role which the believing, covenantal community will play and which the Eternal will never abandon. Here too, in an implied form, is the truth that the extent to which each believer responds positively to the Eternal is the extent to which he or she experiences the fulfillment of God's gracious and profoundest longings for him or her. Yet, herein, one equally meets the truth that God's love continually bears the believer up, even beyond one's failings or the failure of the community itself:

> For you are a people holy to the Lord your God; the Lord your God has chosen you to be a people for his own possession, out of all the peoples that are on the face of the earth. It was not because you were more in number than any other people that the Lord set his love upon you and chose you, for you were the fewest of all peoples; but it is because the Lord loves you, and is keeping the oath which he swore to your fathers, that the Lord has brought you out with a mighty hand, and redeemed you from the house of bondage. . . . Know therefore that the Lord your God is God, the faithful God who keeps covenant and steadfast love with those who love him and keep his commandments, to a thousand generations. . . . You shall therefore be careful to do the commandment, and the statutes, and the ordinances, which I command you this day. (Deut. 7:6-11)

Here, also, is that Reformed, Lutheran, and indeed Catholic sense that the believer belongs to God, that one is not one's own but completely God's exclusive and treasured possession. Within the context of the Hebrew Bible, here is the truth of God's faithfulness, steadfast mercy, and *hesed* loyalty, which, coming first, awakens and then solicits the human response of love. Justification must precede sanctification. Then the believers' virtues become part of a total way of living in conformity with God's highest hopes. The act of bearing in mind that God comes first and loves the believer with an everlasting love, and that one belongs to God constitutes a critical Old Testament virtue.

CHAPTER THREE

Virtues of the Historic, Prophetic, and Wisdom Periods

The Prophetic and Historical Witness

TODAY'S BIBLICAL SCHOLARS believe that, standing as a preamble to the historical and prophetic sections of the Hebrew Bible, is the Deuteronomic Covenant. It has earned this place in the Scriptures, because of its due emphasis on God's electing mercy.

> It was not because you were more in number than any other people that the Lord set his love on you and chose you. . . . It is because the Lord loves you and is keeping the oath that he swore to your fathers. (Deut. 7:7-8)

This "electing mercy" is exalted first, because it is ultimately what the book of Deuteronomny is all about. Here, in its pages, the Hebrew Bible's editors have preserved God's preamble of grace, then comes Israel's response in the form of its pledge of adherence to the Mosaic Torah. Later this theme is modified by an emerging Royal Theology that stresses God's eternal faithfulness to the house of David. Nonetheless, what both motifs herald is God's electing initiative, God's coming first with grace and love. Then the Deuteronomistic historian preserves the human response of faith, as well as Israel and Judah's tragic responses of faithlessness.

This theme of mercy and response is the key to the "virtues" that are derivable from the historic and prophetic sections of the Hebrew Scriptures. Since the Hebrew Bible itself makes the distinction between the "Former" and the "Latter Prophets" (the historical versus the prophetic books), the present examination of the Hebrew Bible's virtues will honor these demarcations.

The Former Prophets:
Joshua through Second Kings

The Hebrew Bible marshals many paradigms of "virtue" in this section. Selecting a few who best reflect the age is no simple matter.

From the Conquest of Canaan to the
Collapse of the Tribal League

Many names stand out: Joshua, Rahab, Deborah, Samson, Gideon, Hannah, Samuel. Each has a role to play in the larger story that the Deuteronomistic historian wishes to preserve. But the historian, himself, is not interested in hallowing the Israelites' virtues or achievements. What makes the above Israelites of interest from an ethical perspective is not his concern. His focus is the fate of Israel, growing out of the people's disobedience to the Mosaic Covenant. Still, many of the period's key persons possess exemplary qualities, but in a manner fitting to the age. From that perspective, Rahab and Samson, for example, are hardly saintly, and, aside from Hannah, the rest are neither compassionate nor models of kindness, of tolerance, or even of respect for the universal moral law. With the exception of Gideon, the remaining three — Joshua, Deborah, and Samuel — possess a zeal that is actually frightening, one that borders on fanaticism. It was enough to make the "tragic hero" Saul (a sometime charismatic of the faith) cringe before Samuel and the beheaded body of Agag. That was not his understanding of God or his vision of what the Lord wanted.

Yet, in retrospect, each of these figures possesses a virtue worthy of the time, which the story more clearly preserves. For the historian of these chapters, each figure was an exemplar of the response that the Mosaic Covenant elicits. Each was willing to be used by the Eternal, willing to resist the ethos of their age that would have nullified the placing of God first. Each was willing to yield his or her conscience to the sole Creator-God, who so stands apart from the naturalistic and dehumanizing ideologies of one's own time, as to be life's true redeemer. To that extent, they are of interest to the Deuteronomistic historian, as exemplars *in service* to God not themselves nor their culture and its values. They exemplify the ethics of both the Covenant and the Holiness codes, within a framework of the Deuteronomic call of loyalty and service to God.

Joshua: "Now therefore fear the Lord, and *serve* him in sincerity and in faithfulness; put away the gods which your fathers served. . . . *Choose* you this day whom you will *serve* . . . ; but as for me and my house, we will *serve* the Lord" (Joshua 24:14-15).

Deborah: "When new gods were chosen, then war was in the gates. . . . My heart goes out to the commanders of Israel who *offered themselves willingly* among the people" (Judges 5:8-9).

Samuel: "*Serve* the Lord with all your heart; and do not turn aside after vain things which cannot profit or save, for they are vain. . . . Behold, to *obey* is better than sacrifice, and to *hearken* than the fat of rams" (1 Sam. 12:20-21; 15:22).

Note, in each of the examples above, the Hebrew verbs provide the clues for inferring the appropriate virtues, viz. *"to serve" ('bad), "to choose" (bahar), "to obey" (sama)*. There can be no substitutes for these virtues, because they form the backbone of biblical faith. As Jesus taught, "No one can serve two masters; for a slave will either hate the one and love the other, or be devoted to the one and despise the other. You cannot serve God and wealth" (NRSV Matt. 6:24). Sincere devotion to God that issues in faithful and loyal obedience to God's will is clearly the emphasis here. Service to God, freely entered upon and obediently pursued, becomes the hallmark of a virtuous life, as outlined by the Deuteronomistic historian.

It is Gideon, however, among the judges, who warrants even the historian's special attention. There is the air of the Abrahamic "knight of faith" about him. He is at once very human, while possessing sound character and moral virtues. When God first comes to him, Gideon does not want to *serve*. His heart is torn by doubts, both about the Eternal and himself: "where are all his wonderful deeds which our fathers recounted to us?" and "Pray,

Lord, how can I deliver Israel?" (Judges 6:13, 15). Here the historian honestly portrays a man who, upon God's initial contact, retreats behind his self-doubts and existential anxieties: "Not me, God! Find another!" Yet, in keeping with his Israelite past, the historian knows that it is this very weakness and lack of pretention that God prefers over self-confidence and human vanity. "Nay, but I am with you. Do not I send you? Go in this might of yours and deliver Israel, you mighty man of valor" (cf. Judges 6:12, 14). And so Gideon goes. Like Abraham and Moses before him, Gideon accepts God's promises. He *believes* and *entrusts* himself to God's ordering of time and history.

Note that it is God (or the angel of God) who calls Gideon a "mighty man of valor." What is his "valor" and his "might"? He was a man of both physical and mental prowess, strong of arm, cunning of mind, and daring of spirit. But, in truth, his "valor" and "might" are characteristics of all persons created in the image of God, whom God has endowed with great potential for intellectual and moral development. The message here is quite clear. This "might" and "valor" belong to all men and women to claim. They are ours to exercise in *obedient* faithfulness to God, to use in love and in *service,* and in reciprocal relationships with all. They fail the believer only when he or she uses them for self and self-power, in pride and vanity, or shrinks from using them as one settles for an inauthentic life. Gideon's "might" and "valor" are translatable into virtues applicable to all. When the heart, mind, and soul are open to God's presence, love, and to God's ordering will for humankind, then human "might" and "valor" can be used to *serve* God's ends and one's true self-actualization.

Finally, there is Gideon's self-acceptance, his uninflated awareness of his true place in history. Israel rallied to this "mighty man of valor," and wanted him to be their king. But Gideon would not allow his personal achievements to blind him or to incline him toward self-deception. "I will not rule over you . . . ; the Lord will rule over you" (Judges 8:23). Here is that *sobriety* which subordinates itself to God, and which Paul will praise in Romans (Rom. 12:3). It does not mean that men and women of "valor" and "might," or "talent" and "ability," are to bury their gifts in the sand (Matt. 25:14-30), or to be afraid to actualize their potential. On the contrary, because they belong to God, it is only when these virtues are used for God and neighbor that they bestow upon the believer the blessings that fulfill existence and contribute to human wholeness.

Hannah

Certainly, the historian draws attention to Hannah, who, along with Gideon, emerges as one of Israel's truly virtuous pre-monarchic persons. From the very beginning, the dynamics of "feminine experience" bracket her existence. The Deuteronomist pulls no punches here. Her self-identity as a woman, and her link to the cycles of regeneration and death, underscore her integrity and anxiety as a person, throughout the story. Yet, what distinguishes Hannah, in the Deuteronomist's mind, is not her link to nature or her need to conceive a son, but the mystery and grace of God, who has created her and whose will for her far exceeds the parameters of her cultural orientation as a woman. In the final analysis, it is God's gracious will for Hannah that fulfills her humanness. Yet, at the same time, it is Hannah's faith in God, her humble acceptance of her role in nature's processes, and her belief that God is not indifferent to her fate as a daughter of the Covenant that also contributes to her dignity.

God loves this woman. Indeed, the story preserves something of that "herstory" that feminists crave to read. For God is the God of women as well as men and there is no distinction in God's eyes. Male and female are equal. There is no hierarchical subordination here and, therefore, no authoritarianism that relegates her to second class status. The story of Hannah proclaims that she, too, is part of God's redemptive acts in behalf of humankind; for she will give birth to Samuel — fulfill her existence as a woman in Nature's cycle — as well as become a chosen participant of God's ongoing redemption of Israel. No man or woman who reads this story with the eyes of faith can fail to hear what the Holy Spirit is saying, that in God there are no sexual distinctions, no hierarchical, patriarchal, or matriarchal preferences. Both sexes are created in the divine "image," and both have a unique and reciprocal role to play as sons and daughters of God.

In fact, women can read this story with pride. For, although her song has been edited to incorporate the nation and the king, her prayer depicts Hannah as a woman of knowledge, a "theologian" in the wisdom tradition, whose "theology" and "ethics" foreshadows those very themes modern feminists seek from today's church, its leaders and institutions.

> "My heart exults in the Lord; my strength is exalted
>   in my God. . . .
> "There is no Holy One like the Lord. . . .
> for the Lord is a God of knowledge,
> and by him actions are weighed. . . .
> He raises up the poor from the dust;
> he lifts the needy from the ash heap. . . .
> "He will guard the feet of his faithful ones. . . ."
>
> NRSV 1 Sam. 2:1-3, 8-9

Her song incorporates those values of an "ethics of care" that undergird an "ethics of justice," and in so doing witness to the sole life-giving God of the universe, who calls all men and women into patterns of partnership, compassion, and reason.

The Undivided Monarchy

This period contains the apex of Israel's past. This is the period a later Judaism would lionize and whose messianic re-possibilities she would anticipate, await, and glorify. It is the age of David and Solomon: one the "apple of God's eye," the other the wisest king Israel ever knew. But again care in analysis is required. Neither man is a saint; yet, in accordance with the story, each possesses virtues worthy of Israel's memory and respect. Once again, however, being "virtuous" in the biblical sense incorporates more than being "saintly," "perfect," "model," "paradigmatic," or "ideal." Only God is perfect — although God's "abstract perfection" is of no interest to the Deuteronomist. However, a life lived in positive response to God can grow in character, and, by the exercise of virtues that flow from character, can deepen and enhance one's existence, both as an individual and as a member of society.

David

Why does the historian love this man — this man so singular, so concrete, so human, and so pious? Like Gideon, he too is portrayed as unpretentious; like Samson, he is depicted as brave and strong; like Abraham, he is presented as a genuine exemplar of faith, and if not a "knight," at least part "mystic" and half "saint." Passionate in battle and passionate in love, he comes to us across the centuries as a genuine flesh-and-bone man, yet much adored by, at least, the biblical historian.

All went well for David, until he met Bathsheba. Then a series of tragedies occurred. It began with David's own amorous advances, then escalated to deceit and Uriah's death. Soon afterwards, David's son Amnon raped Tamar. As a result, Absalom killed Amnon, only later to be killed himself; and finally Sheba ben Bichri led a rebellion that forced the aging king from both his palace and Jerusalem. And Nathan the prophet was there, always a reminder of God's loyalty to Israel, of the rightness of the Covenant, and as a reminder of God's love for David.

Once again the biblical narrative confronts the reader with the realms of grace and awe. God's electing initiative is emphasized first. God's ordering of the universe as that alone which leads to life's highest possibilities is given priority. According to the Court Historian, who preserved this narrative, it is not the community's task to condone or to condemn David but to listen and to learn.

Of all David's finer qualities (faith, courage, trust, kindness, determination, prowess, loyalty, and eloquence), perhaps the one that stands out most clearly is his acceptance of Nathan's judgment of his sin. For the first time the Deuteronomistic historian confronts the community with a person of incredible stature who acknowledges his culpability. At first David is enraged, then he falls silent; finally he accepts his guilt. "Yes, God, it is I!" And his confession leads to that Penitential Psalm the Christian community still takes up when offering to God its own confessions of sin:

> For I know my transgressions, and my sin
> is ever before me. . . .

so that thou are justified in thy sentence
and blameless in thy judgment.

Psalm 51:3-4

David was never too proud to ask for forgiveness, never so
self-enamored as to deny his culpability, never so high-minded as
to be unable to kneel in *repentance*. If Abraham's virtue is faith,
this man's is his sincere and grief-torn *capacity for repentance*. It
is his awareness of his *need for moral renewal*.

Create in me a clean heart, O God,
and put a new and right spirit within me.

Psalm 51:10

The believer is not to minimize the tragic elements that dogged
David's later years. They will always be there. But so is God's love,
presence, and promise, which David also knew to be realities in
his life:

The sacrifice acceptable to God is a broken spirit;
a broken and contrite heart, O God, thou wilt not despise.

Psalm 51:17

There is an irony in all of this that underscores all biblical
virtue and its interest in character: God's strength is made perfect
in human weakness. It is a saving and healing irony, and a paradox.
Again it emphasizes God's grace, that God comes first. And when
that occurs, then both repentance and renewal are possible. Even
Nietzsche has a comment that is worth repeating here: "Irony is
. . . a pedagogic expedient . . . ; its purpose is to humble and
shame, in the wholesome way that causes good resolutions to
spring up and teaches people to show honor and gratitude."[1]

1. From Nietzsche's *Human, All Too Human*, I, par. 372; cited by Geoffrey
Clive in *The Philosophy of Nietzsche* (New York: New American Library, 1965),
524.

Bathsheba

The New Testament will refer to her simply as "the wife of Uriah" (Matt. 1:6). Ahinoam and Abigail provide better models of virtue, for they bring energy, wealth, and healthy spunk to the younger David during the years of his rise to power, but Bathsheba compels recognition. David was willing to commit murder for her, and she, the former wife of a Hittite warrior, becomes Solomon's mother. Her love affair with the king is the essence of universal romance and mirrors something of the enduring condition of human souls.

In retrospect, Bathsheba had no choice but to yield to David's advances. She was a victim of those "hierarchical" and "authoritarian" powers that subjugated women at the time. The king wanted her and it was not for her to resist the king. Her retreat into passivity is understandable. Yet the believing community assumes that she welcomed his arms, finding him as handsome and as amorous as had Ahinoan and Abigail before her. And to that extent, she is not innocent. She could have refused and accepted her fate. So in part, fortune flung her into the limelight in a way she would have never sought it on her own; yet, she accepted it. Still, there is more. It is Rembrandt who brings the Deuteronomist's portrayal of her to light, not because the artist is a male, but because of the power of his insight and art. It is visible in his great painting "Bathsheba." He depicts her nude, having completed her bath, sitting on her couch with only a bracelet about her arm and a thin, green sash gathered loosely about her waist. Her flesh appears soft, her thighs large, her hips and breasts shapely and desirable. But it is her eyes that hold the clue to her character. Softly, they stare down across her body and away into that veil of shadows Rembrandt knew so well how to create. She has come to accept her station, the events of her life as they are, her role and structural nature as a *woman*. There is no anger, remorse, jealousy, or bitterness in her eyes. She has become "the handmaid of the king" — may the Eternal ever be blessed! Here is that Abrahamic sense of humility and trust in God's silent ordering of life that acknowledges that the Eternal can take the structures of being, even the powers of lust and death, into the divine embrace and render them back in wholeness. And that God chooses her son to be the next king, confronts believers all the more with grace, awe, and the reality that God stands at the center, or in Hannah's words: "by him actions are weighed." Only then are life's fuller possibilities accessible without guilt, rancor, shame, or loss.

Indeed, the whole episode of David and Bathsheba reminds us that neither moral weakness nor moral despair have the last word where God is present in human life. There is something more precious than self-respect when self-respect is lost; it is the fallen self discovering its peace and wholeness again in the grace and mercy of God.

The Northern Kingdom and Judah

Towering above all the historical persons of this period looms the prophet Elijah. The historian assigns him a prominent place. His strengths are many and his vices are bold ("I, only I am left"), but his chief virtue is his *resoluteness* in service to God. According to 1 Kings, he stood for the Mosaic Torah in a time of cultural transformation and religious syncretism. He knew if baalism conquered, then God's highest hopes for Israel's good would be set back for ages. He knew when faith must refuse and why. In the midst of pressures at a time when the mythological, nationalistic, and naturalistic clamored for every Israelite's devotion, he knew he had to repudiate it all. For Elijah, only one truth is able to redeem and order human life: God's initiating grace and God's ordering will for the self and for humanity. But keeping God first requires action, commitment, choice, and acceptance of the Eternal at the very inner being: "How long will you go on limping with two different opinions? If the Lord is God, follow him; but if Baal, then follow him" (1 Kings 18:21). Never was it put so clearly or forcefully!

A resolute commitment to God, or stubbornness, if you will, in service to God, is the Hebrew virtue par excellence here. Without it, the believing community is tempted to succumb to the values and ideologies of its time that are ever marshaled to serve an egoistic or diffused self, with its lust for power or corresponding loss of belief in self, whether at the individual or the societal level.

Such renewal requires choice, commitment, action, a choosing by God's grace that puts God foremost and one's neighbor on a level with oneself. As such, it is a virtue that flows from courage and wisdom, as well as from faith in God's ultimate purposes for human life.

In Hebrew, the two verbs that best render the virtues that are requisite here are *bahar (choose)* and *'bad (serve)*. The latter is of especial importance, as *'bad* means also "to *labor,*" to "subordinate oneself to." Serving God is no easy matter; it is work, a labor, a submission of love. Responding with a positive "yes" to God, and following up on that "yes" with commitment and service, are what constitute appropriate responses to God's redemptive initiatives.

Excursus: Mother-Goddess and the Feminist Critique of Yahwism

For some time, the feminist movement has argued that the religion of Judaism is not only patriarchal but its God, Yahweh, nothing more than a masculine, sexist, warrior deity. This has tended to produce three schools of thought: the first, somewhat traditionalist, but at times reformist, wants the Judeo-Christian heritage to acknowledge "feminine" motifs in the naming of God and adjust its theological thought respectfully; the second is more radical, even, at times, revolutionary, and has argued for re-genderizing God in order to enable women to worship the Divine in a manner that speaks to the power and truth of their undeniable feminine experience; the third grows out of anthropological and archeological research and, in the name of women, critiques all Western religious traditions. Theologians of the first group urge their male colleagues to de-emphasize the sexist and oppressive side of traditional Western Christian thought, along with some of its dualism; while theologians of the second group exalt the Mother principle and Goddess elements of pre-biblical societies and other ancient primitive religions. Beyond these two groups is the third, whose interests are less theological and more anthropological.

To this last group belongs Riane Eisler's *The Chalice and the Blade*. Hers is a compelling and fascinating analysis of the "transformation of culture" that has occurred since the subjugation of the Neolithic societies, which were, in Eisler's view, largely matrilineal and matrilocal, and empowered by the Goddess principle. Drawing upon the research of archeologists, anthropologists, and mythologists (e.g., Joseph Campbell), Eisler conceives of the Goddess as the primal symbol of all humanity's (male and female) link with the nurturing forces of Nature. Writes Eisler: "our early ancestors recognized that we and our environment are integrally linked parts of the great mystery of life and death and that all nature must therefore be treated with respect."[2] This consciousness, symbolized by the Goddess, represents a "lost heritage," central to which is the "awe and wonder at the great miracle of our human condition: the miracle of birth incarnated in woman's body."[3] Again, the Goddess symbolizes "the miracle of birth and the power to transform death into life through the mysterious cyclical regeneration of nature."[4] This unity of all things in nature is personified by the Goddess, "who gives her people life, provides them with material and spiritual nurturance, and who even in death can be counted on to take her children back into her cosmic womb."[5] In so doing, she provides the wherewithal for "satisfying life." Thus, working within the orders of nature, she becomes both Creatrix and Redeemtrix. Eisler goes on to trace the destruction of this worldview and its inevitable consequences for women. Eisler charges that the scriptures of such male-dominated religions as Yahwism contain the myths and symbols of this former age. But in Yahwism, Eisler insists, all of the Goddess's powers have been stripped away and either reassigned to the male God, impugned and debased as evil, or denied human access (i.e., as in the stories of Eve, beginning with Yahweh's denial of access to the "tree of life" and the "tree of knowledge," and moving toward the curse against the serpent — always an ancient "feminine" symbol — as well as the increase of pain in childbearing, the destruction of Canaan's "sacred groves," and the eventual total subordination of women throughout Scripture).

2. Riane Eisler, *The Chalice and the Blade*, 3.
3. Ibid.
4. Ibid., 19.
5. Ibid.

How is traditional Christianity to respond to these charges? Certainly, the diminution of the "feminine experience," along with its legitimate symbols of regeneration and power, cannot be denied. Moreover, Eisler's understanding of woman's, as well as man's, closeness to nature is in accordance with the Hebrew Bible's own understanding of humankind's creatureliness. Here, biblical Christianity may concur with her and resolve to transform its own attitude toward women, as well as champion their rightful and equal place alongside men in ecclesiology and all other matters. Nonetheless, having said this, her commitment to all that the Goddess principle symbolizes cannot substitute for that irreplaceable concept of the "image of God," so dear to biblical faith, that requires human beings to be more than mere extensions of the nurturing and cyclical orders of nature. Still, having said that, Eisler's work is commanding and soul-searching, and her ultimate plea for a "partner-modeled" society a responsible one.

The radical theological feminists, however, require the most attention. In all fairness to the theologians who embrace this cause, what is the distinct feminist interpretation of Goddess symbolism that their proponents defend? Perhaps no one has expressed this view of Goddess worship more persuasively than Carol Christ. For her, Goddess–symbolism is significant for four reasons. First of all, Goddess–symbolism affirms female power[6] by acknowledging the legitimacy of the feminine experience as a "beneficent and independent power" (Christ, 277). Accordingly, Christ argues that women are no longer bound to male figures for their salvation and are now free to discover that life's "divine saving and sustaining powers" are in themselves. Consequently, it "undergirds women's trust in their own power and the power of other women in family and society," (Christ, 278) thus liberating them, in her view, from the "authoritarian" and "hierarchical" facets of biblical monotheism. Second, Goddess–symbolism affirms the female body and its cycles of menstruation, childbearing, and caring for the young and dying (Christ, 279). It encourages women to "control and take pride in their bodies" and gives credence to the view that every

6. Carol Christ, "Why Women Need the Goddess: Phenomenological, Psychological, and Political Reflections," in WomanSpirit Rising, 276.

woman's body is "the direct incarnation of waxing and waning, life and death, cycles of the universe"(Christ, 281). Third, Goddess symbolism affirms the positive value of the feminine will (Christ, 282). This emphasis corrects the heretofore traditional trend that has caused women to devalue their wills. Goddess symbolism encourages a woman "to know her will, to believe that her will is valid and that her ambitions can be achieved in the world" (Christ, 284). Christ warns that such a validation does not endorse an egocentric will that ignores the interests of others. Finally, Goddess–symbolism strengthens a woman's bonds with her sister women, especially the bond between mother and daughter (Christ, 285). All told, in Christ's estimation, Goddess–worship enables women to celebrate their newfound beauty and powers in ways that liberate them as human beings and make them whole.

In critique of this interpretation, one must admire the justness of the feminine plea and the soundness of its psychological insight. The affirmations that Goddess-centered worship symbolizes seem valid, at least in Christ's analysis. But what strikes one as ironic is the analysis's ingenious blindness to its own *hubris* and the exaltation of feminine creatureliness as essentially salvific and revelatory. A traditionalist position would need to disavow this feminine exaltation, as much as it would all patriarchal and hierarchical forms of the same.

What is at issue is more than a quarrel over the distinctive natural and rational structures that separate humans along male or female lines, or the corresponding right of either group to "name God." As essential as sexuality is to one's beingness and sense of personhood, and however justly correct women are to condemn males for their past abuses (philosophical, theological, and ecclesiastical), the God of the Judeo-Christian religion transcends these categories and calls humanity to live for more than self-expression and exaltation of sexuality, whether masculine or feminine. To repaganize worship in the name of sexuality, or to deify the old powers and energies of nature, as if by obeisance to them self-fulfillment will blossom, would be as disastrous today as the worship of Baal and Ashtart were in Elijah's time. However inseparable humans are from the orders of nature as contingent beings (as "dust" or "rib"), the "image of God" motif reminds us that all human beings are capable of a self-transcendence, self-reflection, and self-determination that makes them more than victims of biology, behavioral drives, or natural urges and tendencies. This capacity for transcendence, accountability, and self-expression is what makes *Homo sapiens* unique and all they do resplendent with possibility and hope. To resuscitate paganism can serve no good cause at all, other than to jar male and female alike to their senses.

No one has said this better than the Roman Catholic theologian Elisabeth Schüssler Fiorenza, who writes:

> this female-matriarchal language ought not to be absolutized if we do not want to fall prey to a reverse sexist understanding of God. The Christian language about God has to transcend patriarchal as well as matriarchal language and symbols, while at the same time employing a variety of human expressions to reflect a pluriformity of human experience. The truly Christian God language has to affirm mutuality, fulfillment, maturity, and human potentiality not only in terms of gender but also in terms of class, culture, race, and religion if it is to be truly catholic and universal. . . . Women as well as men are not defined by their biology and reproductive capabilities but by the call to discipleship and sainthood. . . . [For] Christian and human vocation consists in transcending one's biological limitations. . . .[7]

The Latter Prophets

The Hebrew Bible includes both the Major and the Minor Prophets as the "Latter Prophets." The Latter Prophets reflect in the same way that the "Former Prophets" do a commitment to the Mosaic Torah, to loyalty to God first, and to the ethics of the Decalogue, the Covenant, and the Holiness codes. Rather than repeat here the virtues espoused so clearly in the Torachean documents, it should suffice to examine selective passages from first the Major and then

7. Elisabeth S. Fiorenza, "Feminist Spirituality, Christian Identity, and Catholic Vision," in *WomanSpirit Rising*, 139f.

the Minor Prophets to see how the respective prophets applied these "virtues."

Jeremiah

His "Temple Sermon" exemplifies this commitment best. It is found in Jeremiah 7 and was preached on the occasion of Jehoiakim's ascension to the throne. All Judah had assembled for the ceremonies and coronation. The spaces about the Temple were packed. The common sentiment seemed to be: "Surely God approves! Surely God's presence can be relied upon no matter what! After all, has not Yahweh established his everlasting covenant with the house of David? Surely, therefore, the Temple represents his fealty to Judah, his presence, and his protection for ever! Why change? Are not the state and the state religion adequate for all our needs, for all time?"

Of course, the biblical answer is "no." Only a courageous loyalty to God can prepare the self and society for the wherewithal that humanizes existence. Civil religion and the values of the state, however universal, practical, expedient, and ennobling at times, can never substitute for a life lived *coram Deo*. This is expressed unequivocally in the thundering preamble of Jeremiah's sermon:

> Reform the whole pattern of your conduct, so that I may dwell with you in this place. Do not put your trust in that lie: "This is Yahweh's temple, Yahweh's temple, Yahweh's temple!" No! Only if you really reform your whole pattern of conduct — if you really behave justly toward another, no longer oppress the alien, the orphan, and the widow, . . . nor follow other gods to your own hurt — only then can I dwell with you in this place. . . . (Jer. 7:3-7; *The Anchor Bible*)

The believer's life cannot be lived by pursuing a spiritualized religion that seeks to offend no one while blending in with the state. According to the Hebrew Bible, the believing community, in both its life and character, must stand in opposition to religion as a mere cultural or civil phenomenon. Particularly within the Christian tradition, the Christian life is more than a thirst for solace; more than a tortured soul seeking sanctuary in the mystery of a

Jesus who exists for a tormented and private self. Jeremiah's sermon reminds believers that God claims their entire life, both their relationship with the Divine as well as their relationship with neighbor. Furthermore, his sermon compels the community to see that, central to biblical faith, is *a willingness to be reformed*. Thus *openness to reform* becomes a crucial biblical virtue, because the exercise of it makes it possible not only for God to renew the self that embodies it but to renew the just and collective commitments of the community of faith as well.

In Jeremiah the believing community is confronted anew with both Tables of the Law, as well as with the *justice* theme of the Covenant Code, linked inseparably to the motifs of the Holiness and Deuteronomic codes. Only to the extent that believers are open to God can they hope to see their God-endowed potential saved from an inevitable and inglorious misuse to flower into that wholeness God longs for all to experience.

First Isaiah, Ezekiel, and Second Isaiah

On the whole, these three prophets may be examined together, for each elaborates similar themes. Each is aware of the majesty of God, of the power of God's renewing mercy, and of God's active presence in history. Consequently, the virtues they summon the Israelites to honor have to do with the essence of faith, hope, and justice.

The Majesty of God

Both Isaiah and Ezekiel witness to the majesty of God. For each, God's majesty is a devastating as well as redemptive experience. On the one hand, it deepens their sense of guilt ("Woe is me . . . for I am a man of unclean lips" — Isa. 6:5; "And when I saw it, I fell upon my face" — Ezek. 1:28). On the other hand, it cleanses and empowers them with hope, giving them a renewed sense of urgency for their own time and hour ("Here am I! Send me" — Isa. 6:8; "Son of man, stand upon your feet" — Ezek. 2:1).

One cannot induce the majesty of God. Granted, ecstatic prophecy had its time and place in God's economy of the whole. Nonetheless, the message of these prophets is unmistakable. The Creator-God is without rival. Therefore, God is without parallel. Their words like "glory," "majesty," and "holiness" are more than metaphors. To be certain, they had their origin in what Mowinckel calls "epiphany theology,"[8] or what Weiser identifies as "theophanous theology."[9] But the value of such words lies in the implications of their meaning, for now they function as symbols that emphasize God's redemptive activity rather than mankind's accomplishment and activity. Their meaning is clear: the believer's life is paradoxically at once humbled and ennobled whenever it "bows" or "stands" before God's majesty. God's majesty not only works its healing ministry in one's heart, but impels one to rise up and to be about the business of caring for others as well. To that extent, the faithful will want gladly to embody the sense of God's majesty, along with the urgency to serve God and neighbor, that celebrating the "theophany" of God engenders. For the theology of "theophany" safeguards Israel's primary ethical presupposition: that God's activity and beingness take precedence over human accomplishment and deeds.

The Power of God's Renewing Mercy and God's Active Presence in History

These two themes stand together as molders of human character. As Ezekiel and Second Isaiah know, humankind has assembled all too frequently at the walls of despair. Who among the faithful has not elbowed his or her way through the crowd toward that wall? It looms as the final statement about humanness. One has come from silence and will return to silence; and there are no values other than the values humans create and impose upon themselves and one another.

Ezekiel and Second Isaiah challenge believers to consider otherwise. As long as one looks only to oneself, one will never know anything but despair. According to these prophets of the

8. Sigmund Mowinckel, *The Psalms in Israel's Worship*, trans. D. P. AP-Thomas (Oxford: Basil Blackwell, 1962), Vol. I, 104ff.
9. Artur Weiser, *The Psalms: A Commentary*, trans. Hubert Hartwell, The Old Testament Library (Philadelphia: The Westminster Press, 1962), 38ff.

Exile, that is inevitable. Humankind was never meant to be the *sole* definer of "good" and "evil." That is why human accompishment should never be elevated to a normative principle. Whenever it is, "failure," "exile," and "alienation" steal into our souls and erode our highest hopes. Only God can be the ultimate determiner, because God has created humankind in the divine image and has defined "good" and "evil" in ways that uplift and reclaim human possibilities and that unleash true potential for moral growth and development, for both self and neighbor.

> Have you not known? Have you not heard?
> The Lord is the everlasting God, the Creator
>   of the ends of the earth. . . .
> He gives power to the faint,
> and to him who has no might he increases strength.
>   Isa. 40:28-29

> And he said to me, "Son of man, can these bones live?"
> And I answered, "O Lord God, thou knowest."
>   Ezek. 37:3

According to these prophets, God is at work in the universe to achieve good. They are united in affirming what the Genesis narratives also declare, that a trust in God's ordering will for the world leads to life's highest good. This providential ordering includes not only God's inscrutable *modus operandi* but every individual's life as well. It includes every believer whenever his or her love, justice, and hope are invested in the lives of fellow human beings. It includes everyone whenever the widow, the orphan, the poor, and the stranger at one's gate are embraced as brothers and sisters. It includes all of God's children whenever they stand before the wall of despair and offer a word of hope and perform a deed of love for their neighbor. It includes believers time and again as beings created in the image of God, endowed with immense gifts of mind and heart to be utilized among their fellow humanity.

It is acceptance of this divine activity, ordering will, and presence that gives the believing community its sense of grace and urgency. In the Christian tradition, it exemplifies with saving clarity what Calvin meant by his phrase "belonging to God," or Luther by his emphasis on a life lived *coram Deo,* "before God." For both Isaiah and Ezekiel, it is the acceptance of God's presence and activity and the believing community's positive response to God's presence that fulfills life and deepens humanness.

In the final analysis, Isaiah sums it up best, when encouraging the practice of the above in the Hebrew virtue of *waiting before God,* before the Eternal:

> They who *wait* for the Lord shall renew their strength.
>
> Isa. 40:31

> Those who *wait* for me shall not be put to shame.
>
> Isa. 49:23

In the Hebrew Bible, no virtue is as sublime or demanding as *waiting for God.* The root word is *qawah* and means to wait trustingly, expectantly, patiently, until the thing waited for is effected. Implied is the summons for one to act in the confident expectation that what one awaits will come to pass. As Artur Weiser writes of this waiting in Psalm 42:5 and 11:

> in a touching dialogue with his own soul [the Psalmist] comes to realize that we are not at all helped by weeping and grieving, but only make our cross and our suffering worse by our sadness. . . . The way that will lead him out of darkness into light is expressed in these words: "Wait for God!" This means nothing but his bearing the whole tension of his life in the strength of a faith which does not see and yet knows that deliverance will not be denied him, that the hour will come when God will be near him in virtue of his presence in the Temple. . . .[10]

God summons us to be quiet and confident within and invites each of us to find strength and hope in the Divine, to experience, as Joseph did, that equanimity which, in the face of hate and strife, enables one to rise above such misery and become a blessing to all. Waiting before the Eternal, or seeking one's renewal in God,

10. Ibid., 349.

is a virtue that God invites all to practice, because such waiting, renewal, and solitude allows God to influence one's dispositions and actions in ways that generate possibilities for untold good. The truth of the matter is, one cannot avoid such waiting and solitude. They are part of human experience as are suffering and sadness. The only question is: will one enter into his or her waiting and solitude, bear his or her suffering and sadness, with "weeping and grieving," or carry them "in the strength of . . . faith" to God? In essence, this is the soul of prayer, in which one brings one's waiting and solitude, one's suffering and sadness, "in the strength of faith" to God. Such waiting profoundly enriches the one who awaits, whose heart and soul is embraced by the divine silence and ineffable healing peace of God.

The Minor Prophets

Five of their voices in particular reaffirm the general categories of the present study. In truth, all the Minor Prophets do this, but Amos, Jonah, Hosea, Zechariah, and Micah confirm it in special ways.

Amos

Once again, the believing community is reminded of the virtues of the Second Table of the Law: *respect, gratitude, truthfulness, faithfulness,* and *contentment.* In all of Amos's oracles, these are the virtues he repeatedly extols. There can be no right standing with God as long as one exploits or ignores one's neighbor, or luxuriates in a materialism that destroys the self. "Let justice roll down like waters, and righteousness like an everflowing stream" (Amos 5:24).

Furthermore, Amos is aware of that pride that substitutes human achievement and human virtues for submission to God and prefers itself and the self's priorities to God's will for humankind's highest good. "I abhor the pride of Jacob" (Amos 6:8); "I hate, I despise your . . . solemn assemblies" (Amos 5:21). No amount of religious fervor, when separated from acts of compassion and justice, can substitute for the acknowledgment and placing of God first.

Jonah

Jonah confronts Israel with the urgency with which the Eternal would have Israel reclaim her fellow humanity. There can be no recourse to God which is, at the same time, a flight from one's neighbor. God's faithful are meant for each other's reciprocity, mutual cooperation, caring, and highest good. Nothing shy of one's best efforts in that direction can be countenanced. Each must stand vigilant against temptations that would separate one from one's neighbor or justify one's "benign neglect" of a neighbor's plight. The neighbor's cry is always urgent and intended for the believer's response. All God asks is that we respond; the Eternal God will see to the harvest, even among the world's Ninevahs.

Hosea

Life begins with God and will end with God. God's *hesed* love alone restores human life. In the long run, each believer is a Gomer: fickle, faithless, prone to inauthenticity, a dweller in life's gutter time and again. And there are times when each knows the depth of this truth, as well as times when one's noblest intentions and actions fail because they are marred by one's "virtuous pride" or loss of self-awareness. But the God who has created all in the divine image, who has made each individual for reciprocity with the Godhead and one another, is not willing to lose any believer without loving him or her back into wholeness.

> How can I give you up, O Ephraim!
>   How can I hand you over, O Israel! . . .
> for I am God and not man,
>   the Holy One in your midst,
>   and I will not come to destroy.
>
> Hosea 11:8-9

Behind the ultimate mystery of the universe stands God, and at the heart of God is love, establishing a good that alone can direct the faithful toward their highest fulfillment. But that requires God first and foremost, who is the beginning and the end. Everything else will then be seen in its proper perspective as each responds in faith and, in the process, discovers anew his or her true humanity.

Zechariah

His appeal comes to the believing community from the context of Judah's return from exile. "Return to me, says the Lord of hosts, and I will return to you" (Zech. 1:3). "Be not like your fathers." Again, as with Jeremiah, the virtue is *recommitment*. Those who return from whatever kind of exile can never return too frequently to God.

This concept of exile painfully depicts the perennial human condition. The believing community is always in exile vis-a-vis the world and its values. Be in the world but not of it. The believing community is also in exile because its own values and source of wholeness always transcend its finite and fragmentary grasp, as well as glimpse, of the whole of time and history. Only one thing can lift it beyond its fragmentary and partial view of history, of life, of the universe. And that is God, the eternal God, who transcends all that is fragmentary and partial. Thus to the extent that one entrusts one's life to God, to the extent that one serves the Creator's will, to that extent one is empowered to realize God's highest hopes. Hence Zechariah emphasizes this virtue of *returning, repentance, renewal,* and *re-commitment* to what makes life sound and whole until such time as all exile, longing, and alienation are overcome.

Second is the virtue of *anticipation*. "Sing and rejoice, O daughter of Zion; for lo, I come . . . behold, I will bring my servant the Branch" (Zech. 2:10; 3:8). In the same way that Zechariah's returning exiles were encouraged to anticipate the coming of God's renewed kingdom and to engage with enthusiasm in the rebuilding of the Temple, so too are all the faithful, especially Christians, who await the final coming and Parousia of the Son of Man, to do so with *industry, confidence, joy,* and *anticipation.* Experiences of exile, longing, and alienation do not mean the negation of time or the negation of finitude. They mean only that time and finitude are never fully grasped or understood apart from the Eternal's will that human life come to fruition now. Hence, each moment of time is to be lived in joy and in anticipation of that final affirmation and total consummation of God's will.

Third, Zachariah underscores the central role that *justice, compassion,* and *mercy* are to play until that time of affirmation and consummation occurs. However trustingly the individual projects himself or herself into God's "time," on this side of time one's neighbor may never be forgotten, neglected, or abandoned. Each person has his or her just and compassionate duties to do. The principles of the Torah maintain their validity. The virtues of *faithfulness, truthfulness, respect, justice,* and *compassion* are still meant to prevail:

> Thus says the Lord of hosts, Render true judgments, show kindness and mercy each to his brother, do not oppress the widow, the fatherless, the sojourner, or the poor; and let none of you devise evil against his brother in your heart. (Zech. 7:9-10)

Micah

Finally, the collection of the Minor Prophets confronts the believing community with one of the church's most treasured texts:

> He has showed you, O man, what is good;
> and what does the Lord require of you
> but to do justice,
> and to love kindness,
> and to walk humbly with your God?
>
> Mic. 6:8

Even the most cursory reading of this passage establishes "good" as that which God and God alone defines. "Good" is what

God "requires," what the Eternal alone knows is best for humankind. And that is to do *justice,* to love *kindness,* and to surrender oneself to that initiating *grace* of God. For God has created humankind in the divine image and endowed all with immense potential for moral growth and development, for transcendence and mutuality, so much so that apart from God and neighbor one cannot experience true wholeness. On closer examination, this Micahean passage approximates Jesus' own summary of the law as *love of God* and *love of neighbor.* On this insight above all others rests the Torah and all the virtues of the prophetic period.

The Wisdom Literature

Scholars distinguish between two types of wisdom literature in the Hebrew Bible, "prudential wisdom" and "reflective wisdom." The first is representative of the book of Proverbs and portions of the Psalms and is found also in the books of the Apocrypha, particularly in the books of the Wisdom of Solomon and Ecclesiasticus. The second is representative of the books of Job and Ecclesiastes.

Each type of wisdom is further characterized by a distinct type of ethic and by corresponding virtues. Prudential wisdom is hailed for its conservative advice, issuing in a long list of pragmatic virtues to exercise. It possesses a confidence and optimism that when these virtues are adhered to, all will go well in a person's life. Reflective wisdom is less optimistic. In contrast, it is highly personal in its advice and is at a loss for simple, pragmatic solutions. If anything, it is afraid to list virtues, or at least too many. But prudential wisdom has no such inhibitions.

The Virtues of Prudential Wisdom

It is largely true that in the Proverbs, the wise men of Israel were content to offer as virtues those tried and true principles of the

Second Table of the Decalogue: *gratitude, respect, truthfulness, faithfulness,* and *contentment.* When these are followed, good will ensue. Prosperity, joy, good health, and happiness, the true "virtuous" person who lives by and in obedience to the wisdom of God, as enshrined in the Torah, will experience them all:

> My son, do not forget . . . my commandments;
> for length of days and years of life
> and abundant welfare will they give you.
>
> Prov. 3:1-2

> Happy is the man who finds wisdom,
> and the man who gets understanding, . . .
> Long life is in her right hand;
> and in her left are riches and honor.
>
> Prov. 3:13, 16

In particular, the virtues that flow from cherishing and "keeping" the *wisdom* of the Torah are reverently gleaned and joyfully exalted by the author or authors of Proverbs. The true "keeper" and lover of the God's gracious Torah will be a person of *industry, diligence, honesty, integrity, moral probity, faithfulness, truthfulness, nonmalevolence, civility, kindness, gentleness, honor,* and above all *loyalty to spouse and family.* With gratitude to God, the author(s) seek to draft a model person, an ethical paradigm for Israel, a fitting moral exemplar. In their effort they create a fascinating figure, a kind of Old Testament determiner of good and evil, but one who is able to do so precisely because his heart has been surrendered to the Eternal and his soul made captive to the Torah of God. They provide the community of faith with a vision of the moral life, founded on the optimistic conviction that whenever human life anchors itself in God, immense potential for good is unleashed. Indeed, we are on the threshold of the "fence around the Torah" that a later Judaism will build.

In a sense, this moral paradigm of prudential wisdom is the Hebrew Bible's reply to Aristotle. Over against his "magnanimous man," the Hebrew Bible provides its own "moral person," its "wise" member of the community and true discerner of wisdom and happiness. Yet, from the New Testament's perspective, an uneasiness haunts this ideal. One detects an embarrassing relish with which the wise men exalt their paradigm. This is not said to deprecate their optimism but is offered as a note of caution, lest one's virtue undo one's source of strength and catapult the believer into the despair of a pride that inevitably fails. As grand a figure as this ideal man is, how different he is from an Abraham, or a Jacob, or, especially, a Joseph, and, above all, a David!

At the same time, one can appreciate the feminist complaint that this prudential ethic, when viewed in its context, unequivocally suppresses women. While ironically acknowledging "wisdom" as feminine (Prov. 8–9), the ethics of the "wise men," nonetheless, assigns women to a secondary role. Again, the irony is that it does so while praising women for their *wisdom, constancy, loyalty, productivity, kindness, strength,* and *dignity:*

> The heart of her husband trusts in her. . . .
> She does him good and not harm. . . .
> She considers a field and buys it. . . .
> She opens her hand to the poor, and reaches
>   out her hand to the needy. . . .
> Strength and dignity are her clothing. . . .
> She opens her mouth with wisdom,
>   and the teaching of kindness is on her tongue.
> NRSV Prov. 31:11-12, 16, 20, 25-26

Whatever the faults or gains of prudential wisdom, scholars today are fond of pointing out that the wisdom writers never laid claim to a direct appeal to God's authority, or to any theory of inspiration for the wisdom they inferred and recorded. It is as if, in this portion of the Bible, humankind uncovers a universal wisdom that God allows all humans to know — even if it errs toward pride or suppression, assertiveness or loss of self-identity — that, in the Thomistic sense, humans might at least have as "happy" a life on earth as possible, shy of direct divine revelation. As such, in their prudential wisdom, the wisdom writers encapsulate something of the universal ethic, as envisioned by humankind, that ennobles life and helps fulfill human existence here and now. To that extent, it stands above mockery or derision. Moreover, it is encountered elsewhere in other cultures, ethical systems, and religions, and has the power to unite humanity as true brothers and sisters under one, Eternal God. The wise men of Israel, however, did bring one insight to this universal ethic from their Mosaic faith that made it unique: their awareness of the electing, mysterious, initiating grace of God!

> The fear of the Lord is the beginning of wisdom,
> and the knowledge of the Holy One is insight.
>
> Prov. 9:10

Consequently, believers ought never deprecate the universal law that reason can discern and articulate in the form of virtues. That is not the part of culture that faith ever need oppose. Rather, what faith's wisdom knows is that the universal can never be the highest goal humans are meant to serve. Only God can fulfill that role. Moreover, one can never attain it "perfectly," simply because human pride and lust for gain, as well as human failing and moral despair, make its attainment impossible. To that extent the universal is not wrong, nor has it ever been. Rather, it promises too much, or defines the "right" in ways that deny others' self-expression and self-identity. For the defining group, it is beneficial; for the defined, it is less so. Or where it does treat all equally, without paternalism, one cannot attain it on his or her own. Attempts to do so end in despair, nausea, pity, or alienation — the tragic "levelers of life," as Nietzsche called them.

Reflective Wisdom

The second type of wisdom now makes its debut. It knows, only too painfully, that because of God's mysterious, transcendent, and open-ended way of ordering the universe — all of which it accepts as good — the human lot will always be marked by mystery, suffering, tragedy, and unfulfilled hope. It is the way of one's humanness since the Fall. For which God is not to be blamed.

Vanity of vanities! . . . All is vanity!
What does man gain by all the toil at which he
   toils under the sun?

                                        Eccl. 1:2-3

Again I saw that under the sun the race is not to the swift,
nor the battle to the strong, nor bread to the wise, nor riches
to the intelligent, nor favor to the men of skill; but time and
chance happen to them all. (Eccl. 9:11)

Yet knowing this, the reflective heart, anchored in the mystery
of the Eternal, refuses to settle for despair. It will not curse the
universe and its moral order. Rather it exercises that Isaianic virtue
(found as well in the Psalms) of *waiting before the Eternal*. It is
from this source that it draws its draughts of strength and cups
of hope, whatever the season, whatever the trial, whatever the
hour.

Naked I came from my mother's womb, and naked shall I
return; the Lord gave, and the Lord has taken away; blessed be
the name of the Lord. (Job 1:21)

I know that thou canst do all things,
   and that no purpose of thine can be thwarted.

                                        Job. 42:2

Here again is the faith of Abraham and Joseph and a mirror
of that intense passionate trust in God as the One alone who
provides life with its true *raison d'etre*. For the author of Job
understands that it is, finally God alone who enables the faithful
to rise above chaos, cynicism, and despair; that it is divine grace
alone that enables one to embrace life again and to love and care
for one's neighbor. For it is God who created humankind in the
divine image, and endowed each with impressive potential for
intellectual growth and moral good, with emotional and relational
abilities, and has blessed the human community with one another's
presence, that all might serve each other and God, and in so doing
experience life's deepest fulfillment.

Conclusion

An exploration of the Hebrew Bible's ethics of character has resulted in emphasizing that the virtues found in its pages are necessarily subordinate to several guiding principles: that God's love and creative initiative come first; that God's grace forms the presupposition for every positive human response; and that God claims all humanity for the Godhead, especially the believing community. It is not enough to wander through the Bible and identify first this human quality and then another and so on until one's list of "virtues" approximates Aristotle's. Rather, the virtues that the Hebrew Bible extols are those which grow out of God's call to faith. As such, they are virtues which are uniquely suited for beings created in God's image, whom the Eternal has endowed with enormous possibilities for intellectual development and moral growth, to live in reciprocity and trust with God and one another. Once this is accepted, then the importance of moral endeavor and growth, and the contribution its brings to personal fulfillment, becomes self-evident. The virtues that emerge in this ongoing process are virtues that not only flow from and deepen one's own human existence and moral character but equally flow from and intensify one's relation to the Eternal and one's neighbor.

In the final analysis, the Reformer Calvin was right to claim the Old Testament and its moral law as "normative" for the Christian community. For Calvin was laying claim to more than the Hebrew Torah. Quite rightly, he was claiming that the God of grace who meets believers in Jesus of Nazareth is the same God of grace who encountered the patriarchs, judges, kings, prophets, and wise men of Israel. It is the same saving truth that reaches out to all, and the same God who would reclaim all to become the beings God has fashioned them to be: persons created in the image of God with incredible potential for intellectual and moral good, whom God has united together in concern for one another's just and compassionate interests. It is God's ordering of the universe — as open-ended as it is — that provides humankind's highest hope and which alone can save human beings from cynicism and despair; it is God's ordering alone which best defines "good" and "evil" in ways that fulfill all. When the virtues that shape life and deepen one's character flow from God's grace, then can one's humanness be enriched if not fulfilled this side of the Resurrection.

CHAPTER FOUR

An Exploration of the New Testament's Ethics of Character: The Gospels

Introduction

THE HEBREW BIBLE provides no definitive list of virtues. They have to be gleaned from the stories and texts, keeping in mind the major guiding principles behind each book or collection of books. However, such is not the case in the New Testament. Whether one is reading the gospels, Paul's letters, or elsewhere, extensive lists of virtues and character-molding motifs are offered. Frequently the virtues are carefully detailed, intended explicitly for adoption and emulation. Paul provides the most exhaustive lists, but they are found throughout the corpus of the New Testament. From Jesus' teachings and parables to the Revelation of John, a variety of dispositions and virtuous activities are commended to the Christian for the deepening of one's life and reciprocity with others.

Nonetheless, even here the virtues and dispositions are subordinate to theological convictions, embodied either in the context of a gospel, or a letter, or implicit in the writer's understanding of Jesus, God, human nature, and the church. In this and the succeeding chapter, an attempt will be made to identify these key principles, or presuppositions, as well as the New Testament's virtues.

To facilitate this exploration, the gospels (primarily the teachings and parables of Jesus), Paul's letters, and the General Epistles will each be examined in turn. First, however, the presuppositions, which the books of the New Testament share, require identification. Like the themes of the Hebrew Bible, they underlie the entire New Testament and shape its ultimate view of character, moral development, and the role that virtues play.

Major New Testament Presuppositions and Their Relevance to an Ethic of Character and Virtue

1. Explicit in John and implicit elsewhere in the New Testament is the acceptance of Christ as the incarnation of God. Granted, this presupposition may belong more to the second century than to the first; nonetheless, its presence overshadows the collected documents of the New Testament. "In the beginning was the *logos* and the *logos* was with God, and the *logos* was God . . . , and without him was not anything made that was made," and "the *logos* became flesh and dwelt among us" (John 1:1-3, 14). Or as John elsewhere expresses it: "What has come into being in him was *life,* and the life was the *light* of all people" (NRSV John 1:3-4; italics for emphasis). What John declares is that in the human life of Jesus of Nazareth, God's infinite *life* and *light,* which enlivens all human existence, has been revealed. In this unique life, God's grace and hope for all humankind are manifest for the world to know. What heretofore could be known of God and life by only the human mind or God's revelation of the divine will to the Israelite people, has now become accessible in the life of Jesus. "I and the Father are one" (John 10:30); "He who has seen me has seen the Father" (John 14:9).

Here, in Christ, is the ground and source of all that defines "good" and "evil," that points humankind to "the way . . . , the truth, and the life" (John 14:6). For John, one cannot come to the "truth" or to "life" by any other means for "no one comes to the Father, but by me" (John 14:6). Christ, then, is both the revealer of God and the revealer of humanity. Christ is the perfect "epiphany" of God's love and goodness for all humankind. Christ's beingness provides that illumination in the light of which all other criteria are to be judged.

No single presupposition unnerves the modern mind as profoundly as this tenet of New Testament faith. Radical feminists oppose it, but not simply on the grounds that God has become incarnate in a male. Rather, what radical feminism rejects is the doctrine's philosophical underpinnings, which feminists identify as "Neo-Platonic," "hierarchical," and "dualistic." For some feminists, these aspects impose a tragic bifurcation upon spirit and nature, mind and body, self-awareness and sexuality. Feminists find this bifurcation objectionable because of the feminine experience that links women so forcefully to nature and to their own self-identity with the natural cycles of life.

Nonetheless, John uses the *logos* concept (the counterpart to the female personified Wisdom of the Hebrew Bible) to symbolize what the New Testament community cannot deny. In Christ's life, the New Testament community experiences "ordering" and "illuminating" powers that, in their estimation, derive only "from above," from the "ground of Being," and therefore must be Divine. Rather than projecting an unwholesome dichotomy onto the totality of human experience, for John *logos* Christology represents a union with the "ground of Being," with the very healing and liberating mystery of God that fulfills one's humanness whether male or female.

If feminists are wrong to exalt the Mother or Goddess principle, is traditional Protestantism right to denigrate Mary's role in the redemption of humanity? Is there not an ontological sense in which Mary, as a human being, plays a vital role in the redemptive story? Symbolically, Mary as *Theotokos,* or bearer of the *logos,* conceives the very *ousia* of God in her womb. In her regenerative powers as woman, Mary carries the Son of God through all nine months of the gestation cycle. The author of the Gospel of Luke portrays Mary as a willing participant in God's self-revelatory and redemptive activity in behalf of all humankind. "Let it be with me according to your word" (NRSV Luke 1:38).

To that extent, *logos* Christology ceases to be a doctrine that symbolizes an overtly sexist, repressive phenomenon. Rather, as a doctrine of faith, it witnesses to the illuminating and life-giving powers of God that become incarnate in both a woman's womb and in the life of her son.

The Son's *humanity* would not be possible without his Mother's humanity; in turn, the Mother's *dignity* is as dependent upon the *logos* as is her Son's. In the light of this realization, neither male nor female believer need fear the exaltation of the Son or the exaltation of his Mother. Together, the historical Jesus and Mary of Nazareth are *logostokoi* — God-bearers. Both witness to the truth that God has become flesh *in* flesh ("born *of* the Virgin," not merely *through* a virgin) for the redemption of all.

As Rilke has himself expressed it:

> Hadst thou not been simple,
>   how could that have happened to thee
> Which now illuminates the night?
> Behold, God, who over all Earth's people's broods,
> In thee descends so mild, embracing the world.[1]

2. Underlying every New Testament text is the good news that the Divine, in Christ, has reconciled the world unto God. It is a reconciliation that flows directly from God and comes as a gift that cannot be earned. It sets human life free: free to be about the things of God, the things of self, and the things of neighbor. It is a true salvation, for it liberates human beings to fulfill their highest end: for God, for self, for others. "For by grace you have been saved through faith; and this is not your own doing, it is the gift of God — not because of works. . . . For we are his workmanship, created in Christ Jesus for good works, which God prepared beforehand, that we should walk in them" (Eph. 2:8-10).

3. Consequently, the old has passed away. Because of the love of God in Christ, anyone in Christ is now a *new being,* whether male or female. "Therefore, if any one is in Christ, he is a new creation; the old has passed away, behold, the new has come. All this is from God, who through Christ reconciled us to himself and gave us the ministry of reconciliation" (2 Cor. 5:17-18). Once again, it is the

---

1. Rainer Maria Rilke, *The Life of the Virgin,* trans. Stephen Spender (London: Vision Press Limited, 1951), 29. I have slightly revised Spender's translation here.

initiating love of God that liberates human life from all that enslaves and limits it and, in the process, directs it beyond itself for a life that can be lived for reciprocity with God and neighbor.

4. Human life no longer belongs exclusively to itself. It is without meaning if it is lived only for the self, or for the universal, or for one's own gender. Human beings belong to God, and, in belonging to God, belong to each other, and, in doing so, experience the deepest fulfillment of self. "You are not your own; you were bought with a price" (1 Cor. 6:19-20); "I have been crucified with Christ; it is no longer I who live, but Christ who lives in me" (Gal. 2:20). "Peace be with you. As the Father has sent me, even so I send you. . . . Receive the Holy Spirit. If you forgive the sins of any, they are forgiven" (John 20:21-23).

Once again, it is the initiating grace of God that liberates humankind, creating human wholeness, and inspiring, in turn, works of liberation and peace.

5. Encompassing the above is the New Testament's conviction that God, in Christ, has conquered death. Death no longer has the final word on human life, for *human beings belong to God, both now and for all time*. As the *Heidelberg Catechism* puts it, "In life and death we belong to God." For the Christian, death cannot have the last and definitive word in a person's life. It is God and God alone who has the last word, the definitive word, and that word, according to Jesus, is that God loves all and chooses to save all. "And when I go and prepare a place for you, I will come again . . . that where I am you may be also" (John 14:3). No moment of personal doubt, defeat, or despair need erode a Christian's sense of worth, or the value of the believing community's effort and fellowship. The value of living for the glory of God and love of neighbor is beyond annihilation.

At the same time, the fact of death's defeat carries an equally urgent appeal to care for one's neighbor — *now* and *in the future*. What believers do has both present and long-term significance, since all of life is lived *coram Deo*. The Christian belongs so radically to God, that one's dispositions and actions shape not only one's own life now but also one's neighbor's life both *now* and in *a time to come*. "If you forgive the sins of any, they are forgiven; if you retain the sins of any, they are retained" (John 20:23).

That death has lost its sting liberates the Christian from both the anxiety of meaninglessness and the fear of death, as well as binding the believer to others, both now and for an eternity to come. That all of life belongs to God gives each believer a sense of urgency to be about the things of God and the things of neighbor. For God has created human beings in the divine image and endowed them with immeasurable gifts for moral and personal good, to be used to serve others.

As all of life belongs to God; so too does all of time. Since life and time belong to God, God gives each believer a measure of breadth and depth that ennobles all moments of existence.

The New Testament confronts the church with this theme time and again. It is a theme that, for the sake of reflection, we will refer to as the principle of *sub specie aeternitatis*. It means, that in the final analysis, the worth and meaningfulness of every human life can never be determined exclusively from this side of eternity.

6. Finally, the New Testament, in concert with the Hebrew Bible, emphasizes the indispensable context of the believing community, which, in this instance, is the church, the *ekklesia*. It is within this nurturing context of faith, hope, and love; within this community of worship, preaching, prayer, mission, sacraments, and healing that the Christian life, as a process, unfolds. It is never a matter of the individual alone, pitted against an alien and hostile culture, that constitutes the epicenter of Christian moral action. It unfolds within the context of a caring and responding community, whose life is lived as much *coram Deo* as is the individual's. Paul himself makes this communal character of the Christian life clear in his opening greeting to the Church at Corinth:

> To the church of God which is at Corinth, to those sanctified in Christ Jesus, called to be saints together with all those who in every place call on the name of our Lord Jesus. (1 Cor. 1:2)

> For just as the body is one and has many members, and all the members of the body, though many, are one body, so it is with Christ. . . . If one member suffers, all suffer together; if one member is honored, all rejoice together. (1 Cor. 12:12, 26)

Or as Dietrich Bonhoeffer has put it:

> the Christian needs another Christian who speaks God's Word
> to him. He needs him again and again when he becomes uncer-
> tain and discouraged, for by himself he cannot help himself
> without belying the truth. . . . The Christ in his own heart is
> weaker than the Christ in the word of his brother; his own heart
> is uncertain, his brother's is sure.[2]

The importance of the Christian community can never be overem-
phasized as an essential context for the nurturing and application
of those virtues the New Testament extols.

These represent only a few of the major presuppositions of
the New Testament, but in their light, an exploration of the virtues
is given a surer context.

The Gospels

We begin with the gospels, focusing primarily on Jesus' teachings
and parables. Since, however, the latter are embedded in specific
traditions that bear witness to Jesus, it seems wise to examine his
teachings and parables within the context of each respective evan-
gelist.

Matthew

Scholars today emphasize that, of the four gospels, Matthew's was
most likely written by a disciple who experienced the emptiness
of the contemporary "rabbinic" tradition and thus presents Jesus
in a manner that contrasts his teachings with those of the Pharisaic
school. While completing the highest hopes and profoundest
depths of the classical Torah, Matthew's Jesus repudiates the spirit
and the teachings of the oral tradition of his day. This is particu-

2. Dietrich Bonhoeffer, *Life Together*, trans. John W. Doberstein (New
York: Harper & Row, 1954), 23.

larly so in "The Sermon on the Mount" where Jesus says: "Unless your righteousness exceeds that of the scribes and Pharisees, you will never enter the kingdom of heaven" (Matt. 5:20). Consequently, Matthew's Jesus lays down a new Torah, appropriate for the Christian community, a torah in tune with God's true will for humankind. It is a torah already foreshadowed in the Mosaic Torah, but Jesus now explains it in a way that "claims" all of life for God.

With this as a departure point, the virtues that ensue take on a vitality and urgency that make them more than mere "idealistic goals" toward which a Christian might aim. First, however, a word about Jesus' "claim."

It begins with Jesus' call to discipleship: "Follow me, and I will make you fish for people" (NRSV Matt. 4:19) and reaches its zenith in Jesus' demand: "If any want to become my followers, let them deny themselves and take up their cross and follow me. For those who want to save their life will lose it, and those who lose their life for my sake will find it" (NRSV Matt. 16:24-25). The New Testament challenges the Christian community from the very beginning with the ageless biblical demand that God must come first. It cannot be otherwise. Paradoxically there can be no attainment of self, or even attainment of community, until the self is denied and surrendered to God. It is exactly the same truth that God put to Abraham at Mt. Moriah. The only way humanness is ever fulfilled is when it is surrendered to God, in service and faith. It is this saving truth that Jesus champions and proclaims for all who would have "life" and have it "abundantly."

At the same time, this claim also incorporates a *theologia crucis*.[3] Take up *your* cross. As Christ identified with and died for all who suffer and are rejected, so the Christian must also identify

---

3. For a useful discussion of the theology of the cross, see Jürgen Moltmann, *The Crucified God: The Cross of Christ as the Foundation and Criticism of Christian Theology*, trans. R. A. Wilson and John Bowden (London: SCM Press Ltd, 1974) as well as Moltmann's *The Power of the Powerless* (San Francisco: Harper & Row, Publishers, 1983), 113-121. Cf. J. B. Maston, *Biblical Ethics*, "The cross . . . permeates and gives meaning and unity to all the ethical teachings of Jesus. . . . It means that the self, with selfish motives and purposes, will no longer be the center around which one builds his life," 162-63.

with and care for all who suffer and are rejected. Even more so, as Jesus experienced the forsakenness of God in fulfilling God's will, so also will Christ's followers. "My God, my God, why have you forsaken me?" is not simply Jesus' forlorn cry of desperation from the cross, but in the final analysis, it is every believer's cry as well. All who take up their cross will experience the forsakenness of God, indeed, the silence of God. Time and again, their brother/sister human being will break their heart; they will feel despised, forsaken, rejected. Indeed, they will *be* despised, forsaken, and rejected. Time and again, their own strength will fail, their own heart break, their own will collapse in despair. And under the weight of their cross, they will cry, "My God, my God, why have you forsaken me? Why are you so silent?" But it is all right so to cry, to bring one's brokenness to God, one's own forlornness and God-abandonedness to God. For that is the cross, where the Father abandoned his own Son in embracing the abandoned of the world. How can anyone identify with the suffering who has never suffered or been abandoned himself or herself? Does not the cross ultimately witness to the mystery of God's own pain of abandonment, which God has borne with silent grace and love since the creation of humankind? So in taking up one's cross, the Christian, like Jesus, experiences a commensurate, though proportionate, forsakenness, rejection, and silence. It is part of a Christian's liberating work as the believer proclaims God's grace to a broken and alienated world.

The Beatitudes

In the light of this claim, Jesus confronts his disciples with a way of being human that mirrors God's deepest longings for all humankind. What, then, are the virtues extolled in the Beatitudes that flow from a life yielded in love and faith to God?

1. *Absolute Renunciation.* It is Bonhoeffer who suggests this phrase in *The Cost of Discipleship*.[4] "Blessed are the poor in spirit,

4. See Dietrich Bonhoeffer, *The Cost of Discipleship*, trans. R. H. Fuller (New York: Macmillan Company, 1937), 97.

for theirs is the kingdom of heaven." The Greek phrase is stunning enough: *oi ptochoi to pneumati:* "the poor in spirit." *Ptochoi*[5] means more than "poor." It means the *indigent* and those who have been reduced to *beggary,* or in this instance, reduced to "spiritual indigence," a self-understanding before God that knows oneself to be no better than a "beggar." If that is the sense of *ptochoi,* then Bonhoeffer is right. The virtue in question is not poverty per se. Rather, what makes the disciple's life "blessed" is the disciple's "renunciation" of self and of the self's universal claim to security, power, and the right to self-determination. It is identical to that self-renunciation Abraham offered to God when he accepted God as higher than the self and the ethical and placed his life and trust in the Divine. It is a virtue that can only flow out of God's coming to one first, out of God's initiative, that awakens the believer's eyes to his or her own spiritual poverty. It is God's costly love that finally issues in encouraging believers to put first things first. As this occurs, one dies to self and begins to live for God. Bonhoeffer's word "absolute," however, causes one to pause. Absoluteness belongs only to God. Humans can never be "absolute" about anything. Therefore, human "renunciation," and especially "self-renunciation," will always remain a growing process. Yet, Bonhoeffer is right to "absolutize" the importance of this process, insofar as "the poor in spirit" identify with the world's rejected in the name of a *theologia crucis.*

The feminist movement has become uncomfortable with this call to "absolute renunciation." Its more radical proponents interpret this call as unnecessarily "dualistic," "hierarchical," and typically male-dominated. In particular Rosemary Ruether has charged that the fusion of Christ with the "transcendent logos of immutable Being," was a synthesis of "world-negating" ideas and dualities, precisely at a time of alienation in religious consciousness.[6] Consequently, its repercussions for women have been devastating, for it has resulted in the devaluation of their own beingness and self-worth and their affinity with Nature.

---

5. All definitions of koine Greek words have been drawn from *The Analytical Greek Lexicon* (New York: Harper & Brothers Publishers [no date]).

6. See Rosemary Reuther's, "Motherearth and the Megamachine" in *WomanSpirit Rising,* 43.

In response, however, the biblical call to self-surrender and "renunciation" has never meant the denial of one's fundamental human creatureliness. Humans remain either male or female, "dust" or "rib," finite, bound to a particular place and time, and to all the exigencies of world occurrence and one's own biological structures. "Absolute renunciation" calls no one to deny his or her distinctive creatureliness, sexuality, or essential beingness. What surrender to God involves is the freedom to avoid that tragic destruction of one's beingness that ensues when one focuses only on one's own self-determining and self-transcending capacities and pursues them apart from God.

The act of *renunciation*, however, is not the only virtue this beatitude inspires. In the Protestant tradition, *docilitas* or *teachableness* also captures Jesus' meaning: "Blessed are the poor in spirit." How teachable is the disciple? How open is one to the ways of God? How willing is one to reform? "The poor in spirit" harbor no pretentions about themselves; they are teachable, willing to be corrected and reformed; they are open to *docilitas,* open to the way and will of God. It is a virtue that Calvin praises and one that the Reformed tradition has cherished for both the individual and society.

2. *The Acceptance of God's Consolation and Comfort.* In the Greek, the verb *pentheo* literally means to be "sad," to "lament over," to "mourn." "Blessed are they that mourn, for they shall be comforted." In his *Myth of Sisyphus,*[7] Albert Camus probes the possibility of modern humankind living without "consolation" and concludes that the "absurd man" of the modern era must be like Nietzsche's sovereign individual, who knows that the self is one's only recourse and that there can be no consolation from without. One must simply be a "saint without God." But this is only true of despair and of a life that in choosing itself over God loses itself.

Christ fully knows how sad human beingness can become in life without consolation. Hence, he first acknowledges as blessed those who are "sad" over the human condition, who understand

7. See Albert Camus, *The Myth of Sisyphus,* trans. Justin O'Brien (New York: Alfred A. Knopf, Inc., 1955), especially the section "An Absurd Reasoning."

the appeal of despair. It is not the condition itself that Christ says is blessed, but the believer's recognition of it. Then, in spite of it, Jesus calls the faithful to surmount despair. To accept despair and sadness is not, particularly, virtuous. Granted, all human beings experience despair, but in Christ this "sadness" *(penthos)* of the human condition can be conquered. There is more than *penthos;* it will not have the final word. As with death, so with despair; as with the grave, so with "mourning." God and God alone will have the final word. Thus Christ calls the believer to accept God's comfort, to accept God as the Comforter, and to accept the Eternal's consolation as the definitive word that life is always worth living. Therefore, one may be of good cheer, unafraid, and unembarrassed to repudiate the *penthos* of the human condition, as well as to reach out to one's neighbors who are in despair and offer them comfort and consolation. Indeed, to deny the need for consolation is to want to eat again of Eden's tragic fruit, by which Adam and Eve learned that, apart from God, humankind cannot define "good" and "evil" without experiencing an abyss of hell.

There is a *penthos* beyond the sadness of the human condition that Christianity recognizes. It is the *penthos* of moral despair, which underlies repentance and is its precursor. Moral despair must not be confused with Aristotle's moral weakness. The morally weak person knows that what he does or craves is self-destructive but is unable to stay his appetite or resist it. Moral despair, however, is more dangerous, for it is irresistable, and more profound, because it is psychological, ontological, and spiritual. It is psychological and ontological insofar as it unnerves one's entire sense of being, of inwardness, self-esteem, and moral worthiness. It strikes at the very core of one's humanness, because it is more than the sadness that comes from a quest for meaning. When searching for meaning, one often finds at least some meaning. But with moral despair, there is only the sense of rejection, forfeiture, a loss of the self's capacity to be taken seriously again, a brokenness too deep for language to express. How does such *penthos* come about? In the truest sense of the word, it derives from guilt and rejection. Guilt, insofar as one's choices go awry and the consequences create pain and sorrow beyond one's capacity to stop or control them. Rejection, insofar as one's efforts for good are despised and trampled on, or one is victimized beyond the power of restitution and the capacity of justice to rectify. Either way, powerlessness haunts the individual and fills one with despair and the temptation to hate, spite, self-pity, or nausea — those tragic "equalizers" that Nietzsche correctly feared. Spiritually, this kind of *penthos* erodes one's relationship to God. It is a cruel *penthos*, whether deserved or undeserved, for one feels judged and separated from God, in destitute need of God's consolation and of one's neighbor's understanding and patience. Yet neither seems to come. It is a true "sickness unto death," for there is no greater tragedy than the spiritual death of one's soul. Christianity understands this. For arriving at this level of *penthos* is the hidden work of God, the gift of the Holy Spirit, embracing the lost to turn the heart again toward the Eternal, the only true human redeemer. Not even moral despair is meant to have the last word, the definitive word, neither for God nor Jesus.

3. *Meekness.* The noun in Greek is *praus.* It means to be meek, gentle, kind, forgiving, mild, humane. Jesus knows that meekness is a hard virtue to accept and a difficult one to define. One can be meek without being Christian. That is the legacy of Nietzsche and his insight into the "weak" Christian whose moral ethic is characterized by spite instead of love, or by a devaluation of one's own purpose and worth. As the church reflects on the life and message of Jesus, it knows that meekness is not equivalent to weakness or resignation, nor does meekness despise strength. Theologically, meekness is a facet of spiritual self-renunciation, of *docilitas;* it is a confident belief in the sufficiency of God, a firmness of character that resists the temptation to make the self sovereign, which might excuse it from having to be kind, forgiving, or humane toward others. It wishes none of that, but clings to God first and foremost, God's glory, wisdom, ordering of the universe, and will for the self. That is meekness, and as such it is a biblical form of wisdom and courage. Meekness means to cherish God's purposes and to choose them over one's own. As a consequence, it opens the earth, the universe, to the believer, that he or she may wander freely in it, as God's true child, created in the image of God for authentic wholeness and reciprocity with one's neighbor.

Equally, *praus* witnesses to Jesus' original ethics of *nonviolence* and *compassion,* of that love and nonassertiveness that Western historical Christianity would later forget and, with the rise of Constantine, would turn into an ethics of subjugation, intolerance, and sometimes barbarity. The Christian must be wary of transvaluating meekness *(praus)* into a form of aggressive and confrontational demand that defeats Jesus' claim that evil is overcome by good, not by an equal counterforce of pride and human intransigence. *Praus* stands in judgment of all attempts to return to what Eisler calls a "dominator" rather than a "partnership" and "equalitarian" model of governing gender interaction. Such *praus* also witnesses to the *theologia crucis* and Christ's call for the Christian to take up his own cross, in an effort to liberate the oppressed neighbor.

4. *Commitment to Righteousness.* Almost half a millennium separates the present era from Martin Luther, who feared the "righteousness of God" and the very idea of "righteousness" itself. For the word "righteousness" conjures up all too readily images of condemnation, wrath, impossible demands, if not hypocrisy and self-righteousness. However, that is not the New Testament's understanding of "righteousness." In the classical Greek *dikaiosune* (righteousness) means "well-ordering." It is the word Plato uses over and over again in the *Republic* to talk about the "best-ordering" of the self and of the state. What is it that culminates in this "best-ordering" for all? Plato concludes that only a life lived in obedience to *reason,* exemplified by *courage* and *moderation* (including, in Plato's *Republic,* an acceptance of women as men's equals), will produce the best-ordered self and the best-ordered state. *Dikaiosune* constitutes that virtue which has traditionally been translated as *justice.*

Matthew has Jesus champion this same *dikaiosune.* "Blessed are those who hunger and thirst after righteousness," says Jesus, who hunger and thirst for this "best-ordering" of the self and "best-ordering" of the state and neighbor. "They shall be satisfied." It is a "best-ordering," however, that transcends anything Plato understood. For it is a *dikaiosune* that put God on the cross. It is the *dikaiosune* that proclaims that in Christ all who are rejected, unrighteous, filled with pain and moral despair, are now accepted and made righteous by the grace of God. Jesus knows that a life committed to wisdom, courage, and temperance alone will not attain this satisfaction, nor will commitment to self, nor the ethical, nor the universal.[8] Both Aristotle and Aquinas admit the possibility of satisfaction from such a commitment, but it cannot (as Aquinas knew) yield that final satisfaction that God longs for human beings to know. Only a life that renounces its own definition of wisdom and justice and seeks God first and God's *dikaiosune* for the self and neighbor can know the highest satisfaction. Blessed are those who seek this "best-ordering," this liberating righteousness of God that lifts life beyond all human *penthos* and frees one to serve God. Commitment to it will not only deepen one's personal wholeness but one's relationship to the state and neighbor as well. In the final analysis, both state and neighbor, all men and women, need this "well-ordering" and so equally need God first and foremost and God's forgiving righteousness.

5. *Mercy.* The noun is *eleos:* pity, mercy, compassion. Jesus loved the classical Torah and understood it inside and out. You shall not wrong the stranger, the widow, the orphan, or the poor. For "if he cries to me, I will hear, for I am compassionate" (Exod. 22:27). "God is love," says John. At heart God is *compassionate* and *merciful,* and, in time, so will Christ's disciples want to be, as they mature in that beingness that his humanity represents. It is a beingness and a maturity that reflects the essence of the divine-human encounter, for, as feminists are eager to emphasize, the older Neolithic societies that were based on "partnership" models instead of "dominator" models were, for the most part, sophisticated, peaceful, and mature. *Mercy* is part of this maturation process, as it continually gnaws away at "hierarchical" and "authoritarian" forms of ethics and values.

This phenomenon of "maturing," as an aspect of mercy, is necessary for other reasons as well. Even Aristotle knew that the virtues, as "habits of the heart," are slow in forming and require repeated expression. One swallow does not make a summer day, nor is wholeness achieved overnight. It takes a lifetime of belief,

---

8. One must distinguish between the "ethical" and the "universal." Universal concepts transcend and embrace particular manifestations of the ethical.

of yielding oneself to the Eternal, of accepting God's mercy, and of growing in mercy before one seems able to reach out and to show mercy toward others in a satisfactory way. Yet Jesus longs for the disciples to come to that moment, to begin today to show *mercy* as much as they can. Tomorrow, perhaps, there can be more and the next day still more. Indeed, for Jesus, *mercy* and *forgiveness* can only be appropriated as one thinks and acts mercifully and forgivingly — for the merciful obtain mercy (Matt. 5:7) in the same way that those who forgive experience forgiveness (Matt. 6:14). Perhaps what Jesus is saying is that, psychologically, it is only in showing mercy that one displays that he or she is truly open to the Eternal. Otherwise, one is deceiving oneself. For wherever one is afraid to show mercy or to act with compassion, then it signifies that one is still clinging to self, with all of its assumptions, and is still fearful of trusting in God or of desiring God's "best-ordering" of life. So Jesus urges the disciples to practice mercy, *eleos,* to practice compassion, knowing that only then, will they become truly satisfied.

6. *Purity of Heart.* "Blessed are the pure in heart, for they shall see God." But how can one be pure of heart unless God purifies the heart? Jesus was aware of this apparent dilemma. Thus Jesus calls the faithful so to will one thing that that "thing" — God first and foremost — may purify one from within, as a pure gift of grace. In the Christian tradition, one can never be pure apart from God. One will always be simultaneously saved and simultaneously a sinner: *simul iustus et peccator.* Or *semper* saved and sinful, as Luther would later rephrase it. Yet, Jesus is right to press his disciples toward a daily hungering for God to be first and foremost. That is both the Christian and the Christian community's only hope, the only thing that can keep life "pure," or whole, or fulfill it in the way that God longs for each to experience wholeness that one may truly see and behold the Divine. Otherwise, the disciples will continue to remain anxious about their "purity." Each will continue to focus on the self, on his or her own beingness, rather than on God's grace and one's need to serve his or her neighbor.

7. *Peace.* The singular noun is *eirenopoios.* It means "peacemaker," one who cultivates peace and concord. It is hardly a

wonder that Jesus turns to peace-making, for he knows that peace flows from God's coming to the disciple first. Thus Jesus appeals to his followers' hunger for God. Yet, Jesus' virtue here appears to be a willingness to *cultivate peace,* to work for peace. Christ wants us to be cultivators of peace, workers for peace, to be "peace-makers," as he calls them. The peacemakers are the true "children" or people of God. For Jesus, peace is not so much the absence of strife — as perhaps the ethical or the universal might define it — but peace is the presence of love. It is the practice of hope, caring, mercy, reaching out, showing compassion, working toward God's "best-ordering" of the universe. It is an "ethics of care" in action. That is peace and wholeness in the biblical sense. Jesus calls the disciple to help bring about this kind of peace, this kind of wholeness, even if it means being rejected, resisted, and misunderstood.

8. *Courage.* Finally, Jesus enlists his disciples' *courage.* He solicits a courage that will stand up in the face of persecution; a courage that will not be discouraged by rejection, despair, unrighteousness, or the absence of mercy. It is a courage that is integral to a *theologia crucis.* The verb "persecute" in Greek is *dioko.* It means to be pursued by someone who harbors "malignity" against you, who is out to "press" you, and who does so with an eager relish. Fallen humanity, even a humanity devoted to the ethical and the universal, is still a humanity prone to pride, deception, perversity, self-rejection, triviality, and even moral despair. Such a humanity will "press" Christ's disciple all it can, sometimes with vicious intent. "Blessed are you when men revile you and persecute you and utter all kinds of evil against you falsely on my account. Rejoice and be glad, for your reward is great in heaven" (Matt. 5:11-12).

Jesus draws the disciples unto himself in this beatitude. For who among them has suffered for Christ's sake as Matthew depicts that suffering here? In the eyes of the church, Christ draws them unto himself, because it is precisely Christ who is committed to confronting such wrath, pride, perversity, deception, and despair. And he does so out of the love of God that he might draw humankind unto himself, thereby achieving God's hope for human wholeness in every believing heart. "As the Father has sent me, so I send you."

Jesus enlists the believer's acts of courage, hope, and compassion in behalf of a "malignant" world in disorder, deception, and despair. And he does so on behalf of the truth that God has created human beings for more than selfhood, or the ethical and the universal, or nature, that we might never know despair. For God has endowed each disciple with remarkable gifts of intellectual ability and moral insight to be used for the divine glory and for one another's essential good. To do so requires courage and fortitude in the face of rejection and hate and active persecution. But Jesus knows that so to act can open the way to wholeness and peace for all.

These are the virtues of the Beatitudes that flow out of a soul committed to God as the highest reality and highest value. Jesus commends them to the disciples, longing for each to experience that wholeness and happiness of life that God longs for all to know.

From the Six Antitheses and
Other Teachings of the Sermon

There are many virtues, or ways of acting virtuous, that Jesus enumerates in Matthew chapters 5–7. One has to treat them as variations on a theme. Here Jesus is not laying down a table of virtues which have to be practiced before one can become his disciple. Rather, Jesus is expounding the inner soul of the Mosaic Torah and its twin pillars of *love of God* and *love of neighbor*. Otherwise, one would become swamped in the coils of a Christian legalism, beleaguered by the assumption that only by practicing Jesus' virtues could one become "better" than the scribes and the Pharisees, and that this human "bettering" is what God in Christ seeks. But that is not the kind of righteousness that "exceeds the righteousness of the scribes and Pharisees." Rather the "well-ordering" that Christ urges is that *docilitas* before God that hungers for God to be first and foremost, that is in the light of God's consolation and God's "best-ordering" made possible through the liberating grace of the cross. Other things will then work out as they should. From that perspective, what are the nuances of the Christian life that Jesus offers in the Antitheses?

In a word they are the nuances of *love* and *trust* in God and of *love* and *compassion* for neighbor. In the "six antitheses" of Matthew 5:21-48, Jesus displays the true intent behind the Second Table of the Law. Drawing especially upon the Decalogue's virtues of *respect, truthfulness, faithfulness,* and *contentment,* Jesus shows how the honoring of God and of neighbor are best advanced in six, concrete, fundamental life situations. For short of the taking of life, even anger and jests require reconsideration. For short of adultery and divorce, even glances and acts that cause disrespect for spouse or neighbor beg for restraint. For short of breaking one's word, using oaths to establish trust is forbidden. Oaths (non-legal) at best represent attempts to safeguard the self, if not also to manipulate others. It is honesty that matters, not what you swear by. Contrary to the universal law of equivalent retaliation — however just in the eyes of humankind, Jesus forbids retaliation or certainly, at least, no revenge. Jesus' principle is clear: evil can be overcome only by good. Hence, beyond adherence to even the universal ethic of respect for neighbor, Jesus proposes *loving one's enemy.* Why? Because this is precisely the way God loves and what God does: "for he makes his sun rise on the evil and on the good, and sends rain on the just and on the unjust" (Matt. 5:45). It is only in this way that true wholeness, or perfection, and loving reciprocity with neighbor is achieved (Matt. 5:48).

Jesus goes on to suggest several other virtues. 1) He advises us to seek out a secret place for the heart's encounter with God as well as the heart's need for daily prayer. Genuine spirituality is a thing of the heart, which God alone can see. What the neighbor must see is one's love, one's comfort when he or she is sore bestead, one's commitment to the genuine "best-ordering" of society. Jesus recognizes the disciple's need for solitude, for one's personal need to hide in God, not because it is an escape, but because in that way do we find in God that strength that empowers our life, sexuality, uniqueness, and being. Such solitude has its place as a virtue when its true intent is God and that deepening of the self that God wills.

2) Jesus tells us to seek first the kingdom of God, trusting in God first and foremost. Jesus never tires of reiterating this greatest need and greatest "virtue" of all: to know that one needs God's

initiating grace, if one is truly to be whole again. 3) We are also told first to rid our life of weakness and perversity before we judge others; then, rather than judging them, respond with acts of love and encouragement. 4) Jesus instructs us to always seek God's strength, God's guidance, God's love in every moment. "Ask, and it will be given you; seek, and you will find; knock, and it will be opened to you" (Matt. 7:7). The disciple can never seek God enough, or knock or ask too often. To think that one neither needs to, nor that God wants one to, would be to draw the saddest inference of all and to become like Camus's "absurd man" — bereft of consolation. God wants the disciples to have consolation, to rise above despair, and to be a source of consolation to others. (5) Finally, he wants us to seek the best for others in the same way that we seek it for ourselves. That is the highest thing a disciple can do. Calvin calls it "the precept of love." "In everything do to others as you would have them do to you; for this is the law and the prophets" (NRSV Matt. 7:12).

That is the kind of wholeness that can come to life when it is surrendered to God in trust and invested in one's neighbor in love. For God has made humankind for more than the self, for more than one's affinity with nature, for more than the ethical and the universal.

Parables

Matthew's parables are also worth exploring, for they contain key dispositions and exemplary activities that Jesus singles out for emulation. Four parables in particular are noteworthy: the Parable of the Wise Servant, the Parable of the Wise and Foolish Maidens, the Parable of the Talents, and the Parable of the Great Judgment. All are set within the shadow of Jesus' future coming and the End-time. All are linked together by Matthew as part of Jesus' "Apocalyptic Sermon" (Matt. 24:45–25:46). The four virtues that Jesus applauds are: *vigilance, accountability, equanimity,* and *compassion.*

1. *Vigilance.* The Greek verb is *gregoreo:* to be awake, to be watchful, attentive, vigilant, circumspect. The wise servant,

maidens, and stewards of these parables vigilantly await the return of the Master, or the coming of the Bridegroom. The delay is not a matter for speculation, self-indulgence, or despair. The Master will come; the Bridegroom will return for his own. In fact, the wise maidens joyfully anticipate the coming of the Bridegroom, while the wise servant and stewards are, with *attentiveness,* to invest themselves and their talents in preparations for the Master's return. And return he does; so too does the Bridegroom to claim his beloved.

The vigilance here is two-sided. On the one hand, Jesus expects an intense wakefulness on the part of a disciple; while on the other, the disciple may joyfully anticipate Jesus' return. Jesus longs for his disciples' "watchful," "vigilant" energy and joy in what he is about and their faith in his ultimate return. He promises that he will not let them down. But they must be attentive, watchful, awake, circumspect. There must be no lapse into naiveté, or self-delusion. Guarding the faith and acting faithfully are no easy matters. But wherever this is achieved, the disciples may joyfully expect and energetically anticipate Christ's return, as well as expect the best from God and demand it of themselves. And they may do so unafraid of the delay of the Parousia. That is not for believers to fear. Time is in God's hands, and so are they. But vigilance is essential.

2. *Accountability.* Part of vigilance is accountability, which in turn implies involvement. Jesus identifies the virtue as being "good and faithful": *agathe* and *pistos* in Greek. It describes one who is generous, true, trusty, and credible. "Well done, good and faithful servant" (Matt. 25:21). What one does or fails to do generates immense repercussions. Jesus seeks his followers' involvement, credibility, their unique, personal input, for which they alone are ultimately accountable. Great joy and good flow from one's positive involvement and *credibility;* sorrow and loss from one's flight into self-indulgence, or from fear and postponing confronting the urgent. Jesus looks to each disciple *to become accountable,* and *to become engaged* in the things that generate benefit for others.

In the final analysis, each servant, maiden, and steward in the above parables knows that he or she is accountable for what each does as well as for what happens to each. What happens to them is the result of what they do. In truth, every human being is accountable for both. The existentialist philosophers are right in their claim that choice is inescapable and that, whether one chooses Yes or No, every person is accountable for what happens to the self. Moreover, they are right in their claim that we are largely self-determined, i.e., that we are accountable for who we become or fail to become. Certainly within the providence of God and God's call for every person to work out the mystery of his or her individual destiny with fear and trembling, no one can fault another for his or her own final "outcome." It is one's own Yes or No to God, to neighbor, and to the house of faith, that determines the kind of person one becomes. True, the believing community may be of invaluable assistance, but in the final analysis, each believer is answerable for his or her own life.

Jesus makes the same point here. The wise and vigilant servants are accountable for what they do as well as for what happens to them. They fully understand this and go about their work with *circumspection, industry* and *pride.* The wise maidens' forethought and action place them in positions of joyful anticipation as they await the coming of the Bridegroom. The foolish maidens' unpreparedness, for which they are solely accountable, results in the tragic curtailment of each woman's future. In the same way, Jesus longs for his disciples' accountable involvement in the things of God that have the power to deepen and fulfill human wholeness.

3. *Equanimity.* We have met this virtue previously in the lives of Joseph and Gideon, as well as in those of Abraham and Bathsheba. It is a virtue that flows from a confidence in God's activity in time and in history, which one's own involvement confirms. It is a virtue that owes its inception to the belief that God's ordering of the universe, that God's will and purposes for human life, that God's coming to mankind first and humankind's yielding to God, creates life's profoundest satisfaction.

It also gives rise to an equanimity that is born out of the acceptance of one's finitude, out of the recognition of one's creatureliness. We are finite, limited to a particular time and place; we are products of particular cultures and communities. Yet, in accordance with the New Testament, this human finitude is lived out under and against the backdrop of an Eternal Infinity, who comes to humankind as Love. In that sense, every moment in time is an instance beloved and made possible by the Eternal. All live in the shadow of the End-time; all are encompassed by more than the vagaries of self, or personal gender structure, or the highest values of the ethical or the universal. Each wise servant, maiden, and steward of Jesus' parables accepts and clings to this truth and does so in faith and hope, with energy and joy.

4. *Compassion*. Finally, Jesus' series of parables ends on the note of compassion. When the Son of Man comes in his glory he will judge on the basis of who showed *compassion* "to the very least" *(elachistoi)* (Matt. 25:40). Here we meet again the Second Table of the Law with its call to *honor neighbor,* and specifically with its emphasis, in the Covenant Code, on justice in the form of *compassion* for the poor: the widow, the orphan, and the stranger. Jesus has not come to abolish that ancient code but to fulfill it. Only this time the stranger, the widow, the orphan, and the poor wear the contemporary garb of *les misérables* of Jesus' day: the hungry, the thirsty, the displaced, the naked, the prisoner, and the sick. Inasmuch as one reaches out to the very "least" of these, one reaches out to the Savior. Of all the virtues Jesus lists, this is the last one he imparts to his disciples, as they gather on the Mount of Olives overlooking the Temple.

The Temple is gone; now believers await Christ's Parousia. Nonetheless, the hungry, the thirsty, the stranger, the naked, the prisoner, and the sick remain in society. And for the church, to reach out to the least of these is to reach out to God in Christ.

Luke

There are parables in Luke's gospel which are appropriately instructive at this juncture. First, however, something of Luke's theological interests needs to be mentioned. It should be noted that Luke's Jesus, in addition to reiterating the virtue of compassion, emphasizes a fifth essential to the Christian life. It is repentance.

5. *Repentance*. The preeminent text is chapter 15:1-32. In this passage Luke preserves three parables that share common

themes and urge repentance: *metanoia*. They are the Parable of the Lost Sheep, the Parable of the Lost Coin, and the Parable of the Prodigal Son, or better the Parable of the Two Sons, one who repents and one who never does.

Once again it is God who takes the initiative. It is the Eternal who scours the hills in search of the lost sheep; who, like the household woman, sweeps in every corner and peers under every bed in quest of the lost coin; who, in the image of the waiting father, takes his post beside the road in the anticipation that surely this is the day his son will return. God's initiating grace always comes first, is always foremost. Then comes the human response, accompanied by heavenly joy. "Just so, I tell you that there is joy before the angels of God over one sinner who repents" (Luke 15:10).

God longs for this *repentance (metanoia)*, as it is the occasion for *joy (charan)*. Not until God is first and foremost, and each disciple has ceased to wander in search of finding himself, can life begin to move toward God's treasured goal for all. It is an action that may require frequent repetition, because, for now, at best, one sees through the glass only darkly. For "if we say we have no sin, we deceive ourselves, and the truth is not in us. If we confess our sins, he is faithful and just, and will forgive our sins and cleanse us from all unrighteousness" (1 John 1:8-9).

Jesus' parables of the "lost" assure his disciples that from *repentance* flows *joy*. There is no shame in repentance, no need to fear repentance. For the Christian, the realization that one perpetually stands in need of repentance *(simul . . . peccator)* is a boon; it expresses the desire to respond in ways that one's life has not yet attained but still may attain. Repentance moves one in that direction. "Repent," said Jesus, "for the kingdom of heaven is at hand."

Repentance, as a virtue, also acknowledges that life is a process. "When I was a child, I thought like a child. . . ." Life changes; so must we. Our way of appraising the self, God, and neighbor may have been adequate earlier, but is it adequate now? In Jesus' first sermon in Mark 1:14, his call to repentance is a call to undergo *metanoia*, which means to undergo radical change. It means to change one's mind, one's heart, one's outlook, one's whole way of thinking and being moral, one's whole attitude toward God, self, the opposite gender, and neighbor. Such a *metaonia* may need to occur at many different times and at many different levels in one's life. This is why studies in human development have produced models which illumine corresponding levels of spirituality and growth which beckon for realization. It is interesting to remember that the Father does not scold the Prodigal for his need to leave home, to travel, and to find himself any more than he scolds the older son for resenting everyone's joy upon the Prodigal's return. He loves each son, in a way appropriate to each, based on each son's level of self-awareness and self-development.

Repentance can bring profound joy, because it enables the self to stand anew before God. Repentance enables the believer to experience, once again, his or her liberation from moral despair as well as to draw inspiration for future levels of reciprocity with God and neighbor. One may now exercise afresh those God-endowed potentials for even profounder levels of intellectual awakening and moral growth, thanks to God's grace and steadfastness.

6. *Social-Consciousness*. Many New Testament scholars note that Luke's portrayal of Jesus is characterized by an emphasis on Jesus' social-consciousness. Luke's gospel is sometimes called the "Gospel of the Outcasts" because of Luke's emphasis on Jesus' ministry to the poor, the outcast, and women. Matthew's Parable of the Great Judgment touches on this, but not in the way that Luke's entire presentation of Jesus develops the theme. This is especially seen in Luke's unique parables, not found elsewhere in the New Testament, as well as in Luke's version of Jesus' Sermon on the Plain and his challenge to Zaccheus. Two parables in particular warrant mention: the Parable of the Good Samaritan and the Parable of the Rich Man and Lazarus. Each is instructive and, though based on the principle of compassion, presses Jesus' audience toward the adoption of a broad social-consciousness.

The Parable of the Rich Man and Lazarus (Luke 16:19-31) depicts an affluent member of society who willfully ignores Lazarus, a homeless man, who begs daily at his door. Jesus displays no interest in either the personal, economic, or social factors that might explain Lazarus' condition, that might either justify or condemn it. Instead, Jesus focuses on Dives' callous indifference to Lazarus' fate. For Jesus, the gap between rich and poor ought to pique the Christian conscience. Yes, Dives should have expressed compassion, but more than compassion is required here. The parable gnaws at the central core of a believer's values and priorities. Where do the poor fit in, the stranger, the prisoner, the widow? Jesus places Lazarus at Dives' very door, his very gateway. He all but brings him into Dives' house and courtyard. It is one's whole attitude toward class and social rank that Jesus probes; who counts and who does not. In Jesus' eyes, everyone is of equal "count" before God; the bosom of Abraham may be blind to class distinctions but not to social injustice.

The classical text for this is the Parable of the Good Samaritan (Luke 10:25-37). In Jesus' day, the Samaritans represented a polyglot people of questionable ethnic origin, religious purity, and moral credentials. But Jesus sweeps all of this aside when asked by the lawyer what must be done to inherit eternal life. "How does the torah answer?" Jesus asks. "By loving God and neighbor." "Good. Go and do likewise." "But who is my neighbor?" And so Jesus stuns him with the story of the Good Samaritan whose social-consciousness transcends those ethnic qualifications, religious boundaries, and national, class, gender, and social limitations that Jesus' contemporaries placed on virtuous duty.

The Christian has the duty to think, to reach, and to care beyond all ethnic, racial, religious, social, economic, and gender limitations. In Luke's second volume of the *euangelion,* in the Acts of the Apostles, he repeats this theme time and again in emphasizing both Philip's ministry to the Samaritans as well as his openness to the Ethiopian eunuch, in Peter's acceptance of the Roman centurion, and in the countless cases of others, in whose situations neither racial, gender, nor political circumstances limit the scope of God's embrace.

Jesus looks for his disciples, whether as individuals or members of a particular Christian community, to transcend peripheral qualifications that place limits on virtuous activity or Christian duty. The Christian life embodies the virtue of social-consciousness, because, in turn, the latter is the embodiment of justice and compassion. It calls for a constant reexamination of values and priorities, lest one's "just" and "compassionate" acts degenerate into sentimental forays into the "mass of humanity" in an effort to appease conscience.

John

An exploration of Jesus' discourses in John is also instructive. For here too the virtues which we have identified are confirmed and expressed by the Jesus of John's gospel in ways that enrich the community's understanding of their scope and purpose. John's gospel emphasizes with clarity that in the life of Jesus believers are truly in the presence of God, the Eternal *logos*.

1. *Sub Specie Aeternitatis*. Aristotle acknowledges that virtues exist whose precise "names" are difficult to formulate. Such is the case here. Two primary texts provide the clue: John 1:1-5, 14; and 14:1-11. "In the beginning was the *logos*, and the *logos* was with God, and the *logos* was God. . . . And the *logos* became flesh and dwelt among us." "I am the way, and the truth, and the life. . . . He who has seen me has seen the Father. If it were not so, would I have told you that I go to prepare a place for you?"

The perspective from which Aristotle developed his system of virtues was based on happiness as humankind's highest end. Virtues which steer the course between excess on the one hand and deficiency on the other guide one toward that end. But Aristotle knew that a "higher" perspective than mere "excess" and "defect" was required in order to enable one to recognize when excess and defect are present. Hence he emphasized that virtue is an activity of the soul in conformity with *reason*.

John's gospel reminds the community of faith that the Christian life and the virtues it inspires flow from crucial perspectives. In John's gospel, Jesus presents a central multi-faceted motif: that human finitude is eternally embraced by the mystery of God, that all of life is lived *sub specie aeternitatis*, under the aspect of eternity, and that eternity wears the aspect of grace. Thus John invites believers to mold their dispositions and actions, not in conformity with reason alone (though certainly the rational bears witness to God), but in conformity with the mystery of the Eternal *logos*, whom Christ has manifested in his own life, and from whose perspective all things are given their final value.

What does this mean? What moral incentive is derived by affirming the notion of *sub specie aeternitatis* as a virtue? In essence, it means that believers belong to God now and for all

time. It means that this finite life, in which God chose to become
incarnate, is not only worth living but ultimately must be measured
against God's eternal perspective — *sub specie aeternitatis*. One's
moments of finitude, doubt, and ambiguity constitute but a frac-
tion of something infinitely larger, all of which God loves and into
which God was willing to be incarnated. "For God so loved the
cosmos . . ." Hence, in Christ, there abounds for the Christian
community "light" and "life" and "grace" sufficient for the living
of all life *sub specie aeternitatis*. The disciple may trust God now
as well as entrust one's future to God. For the *logos-God* is the
God of all time, past, present, and future. God is the very mystery
who enlivens and "ennerves" it. Consequently, as God has embraced one's past and accompanies one now, so will God affirm
one's life in the End-time and in eternity. "He who loses his life
for my sake will find it." "If it were not so, would I have told you
that I go to prepare a place for you?"

Because God affirms life, so can the believer. Because time
and life belong to God, all facets of humanness belong to God.
Hence, because the finite also belongs to God, *sub specie aeternitatis* one need not fear in death either anonymity or annihilation.
Nor does one need to fear the meaninglessness of life, nor its
moments of despair — moral or personal. Nothing one does is
"meaningless." From God's perspective, it is always meaningful to
the Divine, who overcomes human ambiguities and bears humanity
into eternity.

Thus, from the perspective of the Eternal *logos,* manifested
in Christ, nothing one does as a moral agent based on love for
God and love for neighbor, is ever lost. Nothing one does as the
believing community in God's name is ever for nought. It can never
be ruled insignificant, or considered not worth venturing. It will
always stand as having been worthwhile; it will always constitute
a moment of time sacred to God, who, as the Eternal *logos,* is the
sole pervading, sustaining, and transcending mystery of all time,
and who alone invests time and the believer's life with the highest
joy that can be known.

2. *Constancy.* The word in Greek is "abide": *meno.* It means
to "abide in," "to be in close and settled union with," Christ, which
results in a life marked by perseverance, constancy, and steadfast-

ness. "Abide in me, and I in you" (John 15:4). God's initiative has already made the believer clean (15:3). But Jesus knows how important *constancy* and *perseverance* are to the moral life. "He who abides in me, and I in him, he it is that bears much fruit, for apart from me you can do nothing" (15:5). Jesus knows the human need for constant nurture, forgiveness, encouragement, challenge, companionship, support. The Christian life is impossible without it. "As the Father has loved me, so have I loved you; abide in my love. . . . These things I have spoken to you, that my joy may be in you, and that your joy may be full" (15:9, 11). Jesus asks for the disciple's daily recommitment to him. He has already committed himself to his own — "You did not choose me, but I chose you and appointed you that you should go and bear fruit" (15:16). But the bearing of that fruit is impossible apart from one's openness to Christ, one's abiding in him, and one's abiding in the body of the Christian community. He invites and welcomes this kind of indwelling, this kind of abiding in, which engenders a form of tenacity and humility, molded by grace.

3. *Endurance* and *Courage*. A life rooted in Christ's love, presence, and Spirit (the Comforter) not only invites constancy, but requires endurance and courage. At the same time, it engenders the same. Aristotle assayed rightly that one becomes courageous only by acting courageously. Otherwise one is swallowed up by its defect: cowardice. So too Jesus teaches that the Christian life requires a courageous kind of endurance, a determination that unpretentiously scorns one's own values and one's own goals in order that God might be foremost, that God might prevail. Otherwise, the disciple's best potential remains untapped or becomes misappropriated for the advancement of the self, rather than for God or neighbor.

For Jesus, such a life cannot be pursued without cost, without having to reassess priorities and goals. That is why *endurance* is required. "If they persecuted me, they will persecute you" (John 15:20); "In the world you have tribulation; but be of good cheer, I have overcome the world" (John 16:33). Jesus solicits his followers' commitments of endurance, their determinations to commit themselves to him and one another anew everyday — whatever the cost. It requires courage, an inward peace and equanimity that is only

possible because one trusts in God rather than self. It is a courage
that is made possible because Christ has chosen the disciple, because
God in Christ accompanies each in the power of the Spirit, and
because, as the *logos* become flesh, God perceives all things, understands all things, pervades all things, while transcending all things.
Consequently, Christ invites the believer's confidence in him and in
his work, rendered valid for all time, in and over which God rules
from God's eternal vantage point. As Paul puts it:

> More than that, we rejoice in our sufferings, knowing that
> suffering produces endurance, and endurance produces charac-
> ter, and character produces hope, and hope does not disappoint
> us, because God's love has been poured into our hearts through
> the Holy Spirit which has been given to us. (Rom. 5:3-5)

Mark

According to scholarly opinion, the gospel of Mark was the first
to be written. Largely absorbed and repeated in Matthew and
Luke, it nonetheless merits exploration. Christianity was under
severe attack when John Mark wrote his gospel, somewhere between A.D. 65-70. Peter and Paul had been martyred in Rome;
Christians were being torched to provide light for Nero's gardens;
Jerusalem was under attack, if its walls had not already been
breached and the Temple destroyed. If ever "death's dark Angel"
seemed near, it was then. If ever the time was ripe for a cause to
fail, it was then. If ever God seemed absent from the universe, it
was then. Yet, from the perspective of Christianity, the death
angel's victory was denied; under the aspect of God's eternity, God
was as present then as ever in the universe.

Of the many parables and deeds that Mark's record of Jesus'
ministry preserves, four are significant for this study: the Parable
of the Sower and the Soils; the Parable of the Stilling of the Storm;
the debate over "clean" and "unclean"; and the mystery of the
Transfiguration. Each exalts a virtue, a disposition and attitude, a
nuance of Christian character, that Mark's gospel challenges the
community to attain.

1. *Optimism.* Whatever Jesus' original intention might have

been concerning the meaning of the Parable of the Sower and the Soils (Mark 4:1-20), one theme emerges as unmistakable. That God loves all soils and never ceases to believe in their power to yield a harvest, of "thirtyfold and sixtyfold and a hundredfold" (Mark 4:8).[9] Whether it is the hardened path, the rocky ground, the thorn-choked patch, or the good soil, God strides optimistically through the created order of humanity, sowing the word of truth. No matter how hardened a life has become, how shallow it might be, or how choked and dry and wasted, God nonetheless loves all humankind and comes to all in the same hope. God never loses optimism, that eternal hope for each human being and every human life. Nor must the church.

Christ calls the believing community to exercise this optimistic belief in the human response wherever its members go. The church must never allow its own or others' tragedies, horrid world disasters, the base acts of human spite and cruelty, or the appalling social and economic conditions that haunt particular times, to dissuade believers of God's love and hope for each human life. Believers are to mirror God's love. They are to become a conduit of God's presence by their own going out into the world, by their own acts of caring, giving, and believing that wherever the *euangelion* is preached in Christ's name, God will quicken the harvest of hope in human life.

2. *Serenity, Power,* and *Acceptance.* Scholars suggest that the story of the Stilling of the Storm was meant as much for Mark's persecuted Roman audience as it was for Jesus' disciples and their memory of that evening. "Teacher, do you not care if we perish?" (Mark 4:38). So Jesus rebuked the wind and calmed the sea then said to each disciple, "Why are you afraid? Have you no faith?" (Mark 4:40).

In the New Testament tradition, a life in Christ should produce serenity. "Peace! be still!" said Jesus to the winds (Mark 4:39). The Stoics longed for that serenity and for the power that comes when one is able to distinguish between the things "in one's power" over against the things that are not. To that end, they subjected

9. See Edmund A. Steimle's sermon "God's Incredible Optimism," in *Disturbed by Joy* (Philadelphia: Fortress Press, 1967), 131-41.

themselves to severe forms of self-restraint, nobly accepting life's harshest lot, with dogged determination to rise above their personal emotions and private tragedies. But the serenity they sought is not the serenity Christ offers his believers, nor the secret of its power.

Christian serenity is a gift of God's grace that rises out of the heart once the heart has surrendered itself to God. Where God's optimism is cherished and accepted, there too will strength, courage, equanimity, and power flourish in time. Once again, the irony of the gospel is preserved in this story in which the serenity and power that matters is a serenity and power that is born in the midst of strife and disaster. As a virtue, serenity owes its power and possibility to the mystery of grace and the power of one's acceptance of Christ, of faith itself made perfect in human weakness. Jesus knows that to exercise serenity is no small virtue. It means that one can cease to be frightened by the "things not in one's power," since faith believes that all things are in God's power and are possible to God. Thus it witnesses to the power of grace, to the power of God, to sustain one's own life and to renew one's commitments to the highest "good," for God and neighbor.

Moreover, serenity witnesses to that highest acceptance that the mystery of life challenges all to take. In the final analysis, we either accept or reject life, ourselves, our beingness, and others. God calls all of us to accept them all and to live life as courageously and happily as possible.

3. *Purity* and *Inwardness*. Jesus affirms that spiritual character has nothing to do with sham or show. Nor has it anything to do with a moral agent's separation from persons in need, or from persons whose qualities of character are strikingly different from the believer's. The former cannot "defile" a person of faith, for "defilement" comes from within, never from without. As Jesus explains:

> It is what comes out of a person that defiles. For it is from within, from the human heart, that evil intentions come: fornication, theft, murder, adultery, avarice, wickedness, deceit, licentiousness, envy, slander, pride, folly. All these evil things come from within, and they defile a person. (NRSV Mark 7:20-21)

Jesus' warning reminds his disciples that purity comes from within, that ultimately the believer alone is responsible for the kind of person he or she becomes (one cannot blame one's defilement on others), and that no human being's moral, cultural, or economic condition can justify a believer's "washing his hands" of another, as though somehow "contact" with another should make one less of a Christian. To the contrary, it is one's "contact" with others, in the name of God and in the name of their being one's sister and brother, that makes the believer "clean" and "whole" as a person created in the image of God.

4. The *Power* that *Transfigures*. The story of the Transfiguration is a fitting text on which to bring this exploration of the gospels' insights on Christian character to a conclusion. Writes Mark:

> And after six days Jesus took with him Peter and James and John, and led them up a high mountain apart by themselves; and he was transfigured before them. . . . And a cloud overshadowed them, and a voice came out of the cloud, "This is my beloved Son; listen to him." And suddenly looking around they no longer saw any one with them but Jesus only. (Mark 9:2, 7-8)

What is the power that transfigures, that transforms human character? God's beloved Son, the Christ, is the New Testament's answer. It is Jesus of Nazareth, with his openness to his Father, to the Eternal, and with his summons to his disciples to be as open to that transforming power as he was. "Listen to him," says the voice in the cloud. And looking around they saw Jesus only.

Then they turned to descend the mountain and return to the world of striving, suffering, *penthos,* and human need.

CHAPTER FIVE

Paul's Letters and the Role of the Virtues in the First-Century Church

Paul's Letters

It is in Paul's letters that we encounter Christianity's first actual lists of virtues. All are set within the context of Paul's understanding of salvation by grace through faith, which, while liberating the Christian *from* the curse of the law, liberates the Christian *for* a life indwelled by the Holy Spirit. Few passages render it as adequately as Galatians 5:22-23, though similar lists are found in Romans, Colossians, Ephesians, and the Corinthian correspondence.

Galatians

Two preliminary theological considerations provide the context in which Paul discusses the Christian virtues.

The first is the freedom of the Christian. "For freedom Christ has set us free" (Gal. 5:1). The noun in Greek is *eleutheria*, meaning *"liberty" or "freedom."* God in Christ has set all disciples free. However, the believer's freedom, which Christ provides, is hardly a license for doing anything; it is not arbitrary and limitless freedom. Such freedom destroys. As Paul writes to the Corinthians:

" 'All things are lawful,' but not all things are helpful" (1 Cor. 10:23). This is true not only of the freedom Adam and Eve chose to exercise, but, as modern psychology and philosophy attest, it has been true in every human age. Unrestrained freedom enslaves; it is not "helpful." All who choose to become the determiners of their own destiny outside the will of God ironically become fated to experience the worst possible consequences of that choice.

Second, in Paul's view, Christian freedom flows from, and is made possible because of, the indwelling presence of the *Holy Spirit*. For "if you are led by the Spirit you are not under the law" (Gal. 5:18). Following this statement, Paul enumerates the virtues of the Spirit-led life. It is of interest, however, that before doing so, Paul lists the vices of unbounded freedom, which run the gamut from promiscuity to envy, anger, and strife (Gal. 5:19-21). All reflect a moral helplessness, unbridled by either reason, compassion, or common sense. They mirror the *penthos* to which a soul may sink when it is lost in a life lived exclusively for the self.

What are the virtues that flow from the freedom of a Christian life? Paul lists nine.

1. *Love.* The Greek noun is *agape.* Paul affirms what the Hebrew Bible and Jesus' own teachings emphasize. The highest virtue of the Christian life is love. It is foreshadowed in the patriarchal narratives, as well as made explicit in the Covenant Code, the history of Israel, the preaching of the prophets, and in the life and parables of Jesus. It is rooted in the nature of God, who comes to humankind first, and thus makes possible the believer's own coming to God; who has chosen "the elect" and come to them in the Divine *logos,* thereby investing their lives with value and worth.

As a virtue, *agape* both affirms and transcends all ethical or universal understandings of "love." This is especially true of Aristotle's understanding of love — *philia* — (as noble as it is) and of his understanding of *philia*'s contribution to happiness. In Aristotle's system, a life in conformity with reason takes precedence over all else; then come the other virtues, of which *philia* (friendship or affection) is the last in a series of twelve which he explores in the *Nicomachean Ethics,* Bks. 8-9. To Aristotle's credit, he recognizes the joy of intimately knowing another person; yet, even here, the principle of equality (rendering a person one's due) replaces love as the guiding norm. To be sure, a principle of equity and harmonious balance, which is needed to guard against the extremes of "excess" and "defect," insures propriety, but only at the cost of preserving an image of self that cannot know of the higher joy of a self fulfilled in God. Aristotle's *Ethics* is one of the finest expressions of ethical thought, but it contrasts with (though occasionally parallels) Paul's understanding of love. Aristotle's own position is as follows:

> There are . . . three kinds of friendship [based on pleasure, usefulness, and excellence]. Within each kind, people may either be friends on the basis of equality or one partner may be superior to the other. . . . In view of all this, those who are equal must respect the principle of equality by giving equal affection to one another and by establishing equality in other respects, while those who are unequal must make a return proportionate to their superiority or inferiority.[1]

As an example of the universal and the ethical, Aristotle's exploration of *philia* is perhaps without parallel.

Paul's explanation of *agape* is, however, distinctly different from the Aristotelian position of *philia*. Paul's *agape* knows nothing of a distinction based on "superiority or inferiority," and least of all of a distinction based on "male and female" differences (Gal. 3:28). It knows nothing of a "principle of equality." These principles reserve a place for the self, which commitment to God and concern for neighbor have rejected, indeed, transcended. Neither *philia* nor sexual love *(eros)* can ever replace *agape*, the love of God in Christ. As John explains: "In this is love, not that we loved God but that he loved us and sent his Son to be the expiation for our sins. Beloved, if God so loved us, we also ought to love one another" (1 John 4:10-11).

Paul's own explanation makes it equally clear that it is a liberating love that flows out of God's having loved the believer first. God's love has nothing to do with rank, class, or sex. "But God shows his love for us in that while we were yet sinners Christ died for us . . ." (Rom. 5:8). Therefore "Let love be genuine . . . ;

1. *Nicomachean Ethics*, 240.

love one another with brotherly affection" (Rom. 12:9-10). Hence, his definition of love is free of all qualifying restraints:

> Love is patient and kind; love is not jealous or boastful; it is not arrogant or rude. Love does not insist on its own way; it is not irritable or resentful; it does not rejoice at wrong, but rejoices in the right. Love bears all things, believes all things, hopes all things, endures all things. Love never ends. (1 Cor. 13:4-8)

Paul calls believers to practice *agape,* to allow their dispositions and actions to be molded by this kind of love. As such, it has the capacity to release humankind's created, God-endowed potential for moral growth and moral good, not only for the self but for neighbor.

2. *Joy.* The word is *chara* in Greek. In his own catalogue of virtues, Aristotle lists "courage" first and "self-control" second. For a self in search of the ethically sound and the universally stable, we can understand the priority Aristotle assigns to courage and self-control. But where the initiating love of God has broken through the barrier of the self, a different priority emerges in the Christian tradition.

Chara is a manifestation of love. It witnesses to God's gracious activity and presence in a Christian life; it affirms the goodness of life, with all its possibilities for growth and development and inner healing, both in outreach to neighbor and commitment to God. *Joy* witnesses to the meaningfulness of existence. It calls one to transcend self and despair. It invites the world to reject theories that propagate despair, that feed on despair, or that manipulate the despair and inauthenticity of others.

The Christian may be of good cheer, for Christ has overcome the world. God's "perfect love" in Christ "casts out fear" (1 John 4:18). The despair of the modern age witnesses to the emptiness of the search for selfhood that has already declined to consider the Eternal. The reality of God and the reality of grace fill up that emptiness. For the New Testament, wherever God is put foremost and the pride and diffuseness of self transcended, joy will come to fruition.

3. *Peace (eirene).* Since perfect love casts out fear, both the disposition of peace as well as a Christian's outward, active, com-

mitments to peace belong to this virtue. It is Paul's way of witnessing to the *equanimity* that Abraham, Joseph, Gideon, Hannah,
and Bathsheba knew. It is the peace that surpasses understanding,
because it is founded on the knowledge that the world belongs to
the *logos* God, and that no human evil can ever have the final
word. It is God in Christ who will utter that final word, who will
judge all things *sub specie aeternitatis,* and who loves all to the
end. It is a peace that both flows from and nurtures joy, that even
in the midst of one's moments of anxiety and insecurity revives
the human center and deepens one's essence, humanness, and
moral beingness. As a corollary, it strengthens the Christian to be
about the things of peace. It assists the Christian to be committed
to the things that advance the best-ordering of life and community
— just as Joseph did in behalf of his own era's crisis, in spite of
his brothers' vengeance and hate. Hate and fear will not have the
last word. Hence one may joyfully be about the things of God and
the things of neighbor. With industry and pride, the believer may
confidently engage in the day-to-day tasks that establish stability,
that promote and advance the "best-ordering" of life, just as Jesus'
paradigmatic characters, who live in the shadow of the End-time,
vigilantly go about doing.

4. *Patience (makrothumia).* The word can also mean *fortitude, long-suffering, forbearance, clemency,* a willingness to exercise *self-control,* and to refrain from vengeance. Paul knew that
none of this comes about overnight. Although civilized people tend
to extol patience, patience is still perceived as a quaint virtue, if
not a moralistic vice. On all fronts, the drive is to fulfill one's
dreams now; to press aggressively toward one's respective goals,
one's own quest for being.

Perhaps it is impatience that best reveals the positive side of
this Christian virtue. Paul encountered impatience often. Impatience witnesses to a life still centered about the self; patience
witnesses to a life centered about God. Where God is the center,
where God is put first, then God's will and God's ordering will be
preferred over one's own. Consequently, the need for instant grati-
fication, or instant accomplishment, or instant vengeance, is mit-
igated when set against the backdrop of God's wisdom and God's
purposings, which, from the advantage point of God's eternity,

bring balance to the soul. Thus, Christian patience witnesses to God's goodness and oversight of the world.

That, however, is only one side of Christian patience. On the other hand, Christian faith teaches that patience is a form of *perseverance* and *persistence,* or long-suffering and forbearance as *makrothumia* implies. Christian patience has never meant indifference to struggle or wrong, the approval of the status quo, or consigning oneself to a resignation that leaves everything up to "God's will." Long-suffering and forbearance, *perseverance* and *persistence* are also required. For a believer is always part of God's will, created in God's image and endowed with incredible intellectual and moral abilities to be used for God and neighbor. Hence, Christian patience is best seen in its persistent, persevering, long-suffering, forbearing commitment to God and to neighbor. Daily, with industry and renewed fervor, it works toward these goals: planting, watering, caring, pruning, ever vigilant, ever hopeful. It does so knowing that the fruition of the "ordering" that one serves and loves may belong to another to realize. But this is acceptable, for the Christian does not belong to himself or herself but to God, and not to just one moment of time but, in the mystery of God, to all time.

5. Kindness. Chrestotes is the word in Greek. It means *"goodness," "kindness," "gentleness."* But it can also mean *"utility,"* that is, simply making oneself available and of profitable use to another.

There is "a wideness in God's mercy, like the wideness of the sea," Faber, a hymn composer, wrote. Paul invites Christ's disciples to practice this kind of open and understanding usefulness. To do unto others as you would have them do unto you, is the way Jesus puts it. That requires *goodwill, tolerance,* a willingness to think and to act in ways that embrace others within the "wideness of God" rather than reject them out of the narrowness and suspicion of self.

From an ethical viewpoint, kindness is a form of civility and is an acquired virtue that is rooted in respect and propriety. Persons have a right to expect and an obligation to exercise such civility both in society and among themselves. Even more so is this true within the believing community. Aristotle understood its need in developing his own list of virtues, touching on it frequently in his coverage of generosity, magnificence, high-mindedness, gentleness, pleasantness, and friendliness. He knew that a society without civility was beneath humankind. Yet he is careful to safeguard his principles of equality and proportionality with regard to how one ought to act toward one's inferiors and superiors. Superior and inferior never quite pale; one always knows when one is either among equals or unequals (*Nicomachean Ethics*, esp. Bks. 4-5).

However, like love, New Testament *kindness* does not set barriers; it is offered equally to everyone — to Philemon, the slave-holder, as well as to Onesimus, the slave. It seeks to rise above all judgments that would hinder, intimidate, or condemn anyone; kindness longs, instead, to be *useful,* to enhance another's growth, if not change one's heart and sense of ultimate good.

Its defect would be indifference; its excess meanness. Neither indifference nor spite flows from the Holy Spirit. Aristotle condemns both; so does Nietzsche. Rather kindness is a perfect mean for witnessing to God's presence in one's own life as well as a fitting means for expressing one's desire to share and transmit God's grace and "utility" to others. "Be ye kind to one another."

6. *Goodness (agathosune).* Nietzsche defines "goodness" in terms of what the noble-minded, strong-willed, and sovereign individual chooses as "good." In all fairness to him, his "noble ones" always transcend meanness, spite, vengeance, envy, and a narrowness of heart. For Aristotle, goodness is inseparable from all that enhances the highest level of happiness that a rational being can know and do. Both this knowing and doing are essential, for happiness consists not only in "contemplating" the highest human end but also in "doing" it by engaging in "virtuous activity."

For Paul, however, and the New Testament in general, goodness is inseparable from the grace of God and the manner in which God loves. One cannot do good apart from God's liberating love. "No one does good, not even one" (Rom. 3:12). "Wretched man that I am! Who will deliver me from this body of death?" (Rom. 7:24). Only Christ. "Thanks be to God through Jesus Christ" (Rom. 7:25). Hence, for Paul the inevitable inference is simply: "We know that in everything God works for good with those who love him, who are called according to his purpose" (Rom. 8:28). Ultimately then, it is only in God that believers are embraced by that true, singular "good" that overcomes "evil" (Rom. 12:21) and that preserves human life from that mire of "distress" and "peril" that would otherwise destroy it (Rom. 8:35). Because God came to humankind first and chose believers first, one can understand why Paul considers "love" to be the greatest of all the virtues and the highest form of Christian "good."

Paul's own definition of "good" flows from his understanding of God's liberating "love." Within the same verse he writes: "Let love be genuine; . . . hold fast to what is good" (Rom. 12:9). It is this kind of "good," informed by "God's love," that leads him next to claim that "love is the fulfilling of the law," since "love does no wrong to a neighbor" (Rom. 13:10).

In the final analysis, this is the most fitting definition for what "goodness" is all about. *Goodness* is so to love a neighbor as to eschew every choice that would bring that neighbor harm, that would bring him or her wrong, or that would separate the neighbor from the love of God. In fact, as the *logos* become flesh, the humanity of Christ becomes, itself, the highest good and final norm for all "good" that a Christian can contemplate or do.

There is a parallelism here between Paul and Aristotle, insofar as Christian goodness also involves knowing and doing. For the virtue of goodness consists both in knowing it to be a form of God's love as well as a suitable activity in which God urges believers to become engaged. For the practice of it not only deepens one's personal and moral selfhood but equally contributes to a neighbor's wholeness.

7. *Faithfulness (pistis)*. It can also mean *"honesty," "truthfulness,"* or "to be *of firm persuasion."* It is a universal ethical virtue and is embodied in every civilized code desirous of creating goodwill and respect among its peoples. The British philosopher W. D. Ross refers to *faithfulness* under the category of "fidelity" and identifies it as a *prima facie* duty.[2] *Prima facie* (Latin meaning "on first appearance") duties are self-evident acts which are intuitively grasped by the mind as the right or fitting things to be done in most situations. Foremost among them is "fidelity." We all sense

2. See William David Ross, *The Right and the Good* (Oxford: Clarendon Press, 1930), 19f.

the importance of keeping promises, of not lying, of honoring our word. Faithfulness, in this universal sense, is an essential component of moral humanity and is as old as any characteristic of human good.

Paul calls upon the believing community also to exercise and practice this minimal universal principle. But the Christian concept of *faithfulness* is rooted in more than the ethical and the universal. To say so is not to denigrate the ethical, which itself witnesses to what is rationally knowable of God's universal moral law, but to underscore the biblical realization that Christian faithfulness both flows from and is nurtured by that *hesed* faithfulness of God's loyalty and steadfastness, by means of which God, in the Old Testament, constantly remains "faithful" to Israel and, in the New, repledges that faithfulness to the church. Consequently, God elicits one's *constancy, firmness of persuasion,* and *faithfulness,* in return. "Abide in me and I in you. . . . He who abides in me, and I in him, he it is that bears much fruit, for apart from me you can do nothing" (John 15:4-5). Even if one's hearts condemns one, "God is greater than our hearts" (1 John 3:20) and ever renews the Divine faithfulness to believers.

Nurtured by God's faithfulness, Christians too, as individuals and members of the believing community, can grow in faithfulness and in fidelity to others. Knowing that God never breaks promise with the "elect," each can find solace and strength in God when betrayed by others. Finally, nurtured by God's faithfulness, each can recommit his or her own pledges of loyalty to God and neighbor, free of rancor and spite. For faithfulness overcomes spite. Or as Paul rephrases it: "let us not grow weary in well-doing, for in due season we shall reap, if we do not lose heart. So then, . . . let us do good to all . . ." (Gal. 6:9-10).

8. *Gentleness.* The word in Greek is *prautes;* it can mean *meekness, mildness, forbearance, gentleness, kindness.* Even Aristotle knows of this *prautes* or "gentleness"; it is his mean between the excess of "short-temperedness" and the defect of "apathy." The excess in particular concerned him. He associates it with "anger," aimed at "the wrong persons, under the wrong circumstances, to an improper degree, too quickly, and for an unduly long time."[3]

3. *Nichomachean Ethics,* 101.

Aristotle knows there are times when "righteous indignation" has
its place; but otherwise, gentleness is by far the more preferable
virtue to exercise. He says it so well: "a gentle person is forgiving
rather than vindictive. . . . Sullen people are hard to appease and
their anger lasts for a long time."[4]

Once again, at a minimum, Paul encourages the church to
rise above impatience, short-temperedness, sullenness, and anger.
These "qualities" still characterize a life centered about self rather
than God. God, on the contrary, woos believers away from them.
He renews the faithful by his own patient, long-suffering, forgiving,
and forbearing Spirit to become more nearly and more daily the
men and women whom God has created them to be.

9. *Self-Control. Egkrateia: self-control, continence, temperance.* Finally, Paul enunciates the last virtue in this list. Aristotle
made it his second, following courage. For the latter, it takes an
incredible amount of courage, enlightened by wisdom, to rise
above self-indulgence and insensitivity and practice self-control in
all areas of life. Those who succeed are morally strong; those who
fail display "moral weakness" and can never experience true happiness or the highest human good.

In an ethical system in which one's own moral effort either
gains or loses one the highest good, courage and self-control are
essential; they are first and require practice and attention. But, for
Paul, the Christian's highest good transcends this self-achieved
happiness. On his own, the Christian can never fulfill it perfectly,
unselfishly, without anxiety or uncertainty. The Christian is forever
semper iustus et peccator. This insight of Paul's and Luther's
forever places the Christian in tension with the universal or the
purely ethical. At heart, the Christian's life is always lived *coram
Deo,* "in the presence of God." He is not his own, but belongs to
God.

Paul is not hesitant to repeat this note time and again, because
it reclaims believers from every effort to save themselves. Paul
longs for the faithful to exercise "self-control," continence, temperance, to crucify "the flesh with its passions and desires" (Gal. 5:24).
But he knows that even this is the work of the Holy Spirit, who

4. Ibid.

comforts believers and leads them forward day to day. This in no way mitigates the importance of "self-control." But the most self-controlled person, especially a Christian, must never suppose that his virtue of "self-control" is what makes him whole in the Christian sense.

In the final analysis, Paul emphasizes that self-control is subordinate to the virtue of love. One is to love God with all the heart, with all the mind, and with all one's strength, and one's neighbor as oneself. For the Christian the focus can never be on one's own "self-control." It is God's controlling presence in one's life that frees the believer from his or her "wretchedness," as Paul puts it, and makes possible his or her genuine commitments of self to God and neighbor. It is this controlling and joyfully liberating presence of God that Paul longs for all to know and act upon. When love of God and love of neighbor are given their due, then one will want to rise above "self-indulgence" because of the love of God in one's heart. But to think of it as a virtuous work that enhances the self begs the question.

Romans

Galatians contains other verses that, if pressed, provide additional virtues. Paul's letter to the Romans, however, offers additional lists of virtues. Chapter 12 is where we find them.

1. *The Renewal of One's Mind.* "Do not be conformed to this world but be transformed by the renewal of your mind *(anakainosei tou noos)*, that you may prove what is the will *(thelema)* of God, what is good and acceptable and perfect" (Rom. 12:2). Here the "good" is clearly equivalent to "God's will." Humankind's highest good and perfection is inseparable from God's highest willed vision of the same. To move toward that will requires repentance and the renewal of the *noos:* that human center of reasoning and discerning that can and does direct human action. It, too, must be recommitted to the things of God. It is the New Testament's source for Augustine's "I believe in order to understand."

Paul's claim in Romans is that to be open to such renewal

is essential for the Christian life. It involves that call to *docilitas* and absolute denial of which Jesus spoke in the first Beatitude, of accepting one's "spiritual indigence." It incorporates that "returning to the Lord" that Jeremiah begged Jehoiakim's era to consider, but which it would not. It is only by the renewal of the mind in recommitment to the things of God and the things of neighbor that lives are lifted above the tragic and vengeful dimensions that often characterize the highest ethical efforts of "this world." Thus Paul calls upon Christians to *renew* their minds.

2. *Humility.* The virtue here is *sober-minded self-awareness.* "I say to everyone among you not to think of yourself more highly than you ought to think, but to think with sober judgment *(sophronein),* each according to the measure of faith that God has assigned" (NRSV Rom. 12:3).

Paul is certainly not embarrassed by the idea of *sophroneo,* which means "to be of a sound mind," calm, sober, sedate. It is not inappropriate for Christians to be "sedate" in the sense of being sober-minded, aware of that alone which ennerves their center of being. From such *sober-minded self-awareness* comes humility, which Paul praises throughout his writings: "In humility count others better than yourselves" (Phil. 2:3). Elsewhere he commends the virtue of "lowliness" (Eph. 4:2; Col. 3:12). Such are possible where a *sober-minded self-awareness* serves to keep one open to God and others.

Even Nietzsche, that most misunderstood and maligned philosopher of the nineteenth century, was not opposed to such sober-minded self-awareness, or humility. In his comment on "irony" and its place in pedagogy, he writes: "its purpose is to humble and to shame, but in the wholesome way that causes good resolutions to spring up and teaches people to show honor and gratitude."[5]

Sober-minded self-awareness is a fitting Christian virtue. It is fitting because it encourages believers to show honor and gratitude to all to whom honor and gratitude are due. It is fitting because in a wholesome way it enjoins each Christian to strive for a sober,

5. Nietzsche, *All too Human,* cited by Clive, *The Philosophy of Nietzsche,* 524.

realistic view of the self. It reminds us that since the self belongs to God, it has no grounds on which to boast, other than the grounds of God's mercy and grace. Hence, Paul's call to humility and *sophronein* undercuts the human inclination toward arrogance and any form of haughtiness. "Do not be haughty, but associate with the lowly; never be conceited" (Rom. 12:16). There is no shame in humility, because it has the power to cause "good resolutions to spring up" and renew commitments to God and neighbor.

It is interesting to note that Aristotle considers humility to be a deficiency. While he applauds truthfulness, he deplores its excess, "boastfulness," and its defect, "self-depreciation." The virtuous person rises above the temptation to think "too lowly" of himself or to engage in "self-deprecation."

Even Paul does not call for "self-disapproval," or "self-deprecation," or the "devaluation of the self." Rather, one is to think of oneself with "sober judgment." No one is to place himself or herself above another; yet neither should anyone disparage the unique gifts God has given each believer. The context of this "sober judgment" comes within Paul's invitation for each to use his or her "gift" with diligence, joyfulness, and faithfulness. That requires sobriety and humility, but in "the wholesome way," in order that one's gifts might, all the more, be used for the glory of God and love of neighbor.

3. *Zeal.* Paul now inundates the Roman community with a catalog of virtuous attitudes and actions which flow appropriately out of a Christian's renewal of mind and sober self-awareness. Our study lists them here in a kind of silent wonderment:

> Never flag in zeal.
> Be aglow with the Spirit.
> Serve the Lord.
> Rejoice in your hope.
> Be patient in tribulation.
> Be constant in prayer.
> Contribute to the needs of the saints.
> Practice hospitality.
> Bless those who persecute you.
> Rejoice with those who rejoice.

Weep with those who weep.
Live in harmony with one another.
Repay no one evil for evil.
Live peaceably with all.

                                                    Rom. 12:11-18

It is an imposing list. One can understand why Luther insisted that Jesus comes not as a "lawgiver" but as a "forgiver of sins." Yet, even for Paul, these virtuous dispositions and actions can grow only out of a soul whose mind and heart are daily being renewed by the power of God's love. They can only be engendered in one to the extent that, in sober-minded self-awareness, a believer is willing for God's indwelling grace to pervade and mold one's center of being.

In Pauline theology, the above is precisely what God wants to do and longs for each Christian to experience. Therefore, Paul presses forward with his list. The Christian life is possible because of God's grace and mercy and because of the presence of Christ's Spirit in a believer's heart. Since God has already claimed believers for the Divine and has come to them first, there can be no fear of God's rejection. On the contrary, freed by God's love, a believer is now free to live in God's love and to act out of that love toward his or her neighbor. Thus God seeks the Christian's zeal *(spoude)*, his or her diligent and earnest application of self for God and neighbor. God solicits the believer's energetic involvement and encourages one's participation. For Paul knows that one's own involvement will add to that wholeness and sense of well-being that God invites all to discover and accept. So he balances the wonder with zeal, just as Jesus' paradigmatic wise servants, maidens, and stewards joyfully do.

The Corinthian Correspondence

Passages in Ephesians, Philippians, and Colossians provide similar catalogs of virtues, an examination of which would be redundant. The Corinthian correspondence, however, produces three distinct virtues that are worthy of exploration. The first is found in 1 Corinthians 12:7, 12-26; the second in 1 Corinthians 13:9-13 and 2 Corinthians 4:7; and the third in 2 Corinthians 5:16-21.

1. *The Place of Community.* Paul never ceases to emphasize the role of the believing community. For the Apostle, the Christian life is not meant to function outside the bounds of relationships or proceed apart from the communal and interpersonal resources of the believing *ekklesia*. Even monks and nuns belong to orders that sustain them. Eisler's *The Chalice and the Blade* pleads for such "partnership" and "transformational" caring, that is neither patriarchal nor matriarchal, but is mutually supportive. Paul writes:

> To each is given the manifestation of the Spirit for the common good. . . . For just as the body is one and has many members . . . , so it is with Christ. (1 Cor. 12:7, 12)

Each Christian needs a fellow Christian. It is a Christian virtue both to acknowledge this as well as to seek and practice community. Each needs to be a participant in the believing fellowship, in its worship, preaching, sacraments, teaching, nurturing, mission, and works of love.

2. *Hope and the Aspect of Eternity.* Paul reminds the community that believers are bound by time and place, that they are creatures of culture and circumstance, and governed by the stages of personal development. "When I was a child, I spoke like a child. . . ." This is part of creatureliness, which is characteristic of all humanness created in God's image, whether "out of the dust of the earth" or "the rib" of one's partner.

Time is divided into past, present, and future. The past can be recorded and remembered; the present is always fleeting; the future at best can only be anticipated. For this reason the Christian needs *hope.* God's love in Christ frees one from the past in order that one might serve God now and in the future. In so doing God becomes one's ground of hope. But that future is always characterized by uncertainty and mystery and anticipated with anxiety, even within the believing community. Therefore, uncertainty, mystery, and anxiety constitute part of the human anticipation of the future, which yields at best only a fragmentary glance into time. Paul sums it up in his statement: "now we see in a mirror dimly. . . . Now I know in part" (1 Cor. 13:12).

Paul's point, however, is that this fragmentary quality of life, so anchored in time and obscure and uncertain as to the future, need never unnerve the believer or deter him or her from virtuous activity, whether personal or communal. One is to take *hope* and to exercise *love*. The fact that Christians "have this treasure in earthen vessels" shows only "that the transcendent power belongs to God" and not to them (2 Cor. 4:7).

Once again believers are confronted by the mystery of life as something to be lived *sub specie aeternitatis*. That one cannot know what the future may hold belongs to the phenomenon of human existence as God has willed it. But, far to the contrary, this factor poses no cause for despair. For God, who sees everything from the aspect of eternity, is still the loving, Eternal God, from whom nothing can separate a believer in Christ. Now one may know only "in part," but "then [one] shall understand fully, even as [one] has been fully understood." This is the Christian ground for hope. The believer does not have to understand it all to understand that love of God and love of neighbor are what sustain existence.

3. *Reconciliation.* "So we are ambassadors for Christ, God making his appeal through us" (2 Cor. 5:20). For Paul, the precariousness of human existence never erodes the certainty of God's grace and presence, nor can it undermine the optimism God shows toward believers. Of the many optimists in the Bible, God surpasses them all. God chooses to invest continuous confidence in the human response, as well as to exercise patience in enlisting individual Christians and the believing community in the divine cause.

In spite of one's own anxieties this side of eternity, God invites all to trust the divine purpose and presence and to become reconcilers in God's world. From God's side of eternity, God has reconciled the world; thus, the Christian too may become engaged in ministries of reconciliation.

This is done by not putting "obstacle(s) in any one's way" (2 Cor. 6:3) and by personal commitments to dispositions and actions which display "purity, knowledge, forbearance, kindness, the Holy Spirit, genuine love, truthful speech, and the power of God" (2 Cor. 6:6-7).

It is what the community does "working together with him"

(2 Cor. 6:1). From this side of eternity, the believer may draw strength from the power of God's constancy and mercy. Therefore, as ambassadors of Christ, whatever "afflictions, hardships, calamities, . . . tumults, labors," and "watching(s)" the Christian may encounter, all can be "endured" because of God's grace and commitment to the *ekklesia* (2 Cor. 6:4-5).

Ephesians

Finally, among letters inspired by Pauline theology, is Ephesians, with its emphasis on a variety of virtues that extol marriage, the home, and family. As the New Testament scholar A. M. Hunter notes, "Paul's concept of subordination is not popular in these days when we never tire of affirming that all men are created equal and when there is much talk of the equality of the sexes."[6] Yet, Hunter explains, the central theme of Ephesians is "unity," and it is this theme that guides readers through the "hierarchical" rankings encountered there.

In Ephesians, the central values are *unity, commitment, partnership,* and *love.* All four combine to deepen the resources required to sustain marriage, as well as nurture and reinforce mutuality, trust, and self-giving, the inescapable facets of the nuptial bonds. The mutuality sought derives from a loving and caring self-subordination, inspired by Christ, that desires to put the spouse on the same priority level as the self. As Ephesians extols: "Be subject to one another out of reverence for Christ" (NRSV Eph. 5:21). Note that, in this preface, the emphasis falls on equalitarian attitudes and dispositions. There are no hierarchical, authoritarian, or repressive orders sanctioned in this preface. Both male and female are "subject to one another." In the marriage, neither takes priority over the other. Then, in acknowledgment of a marriage's need for bone-deep solidarity (Gen. 2:24), wives are called to be "subject" to husbands and husbands commanded to "love" their wives. Both "calls" and "commands" are based on

6. A. M. Hunter, *The Layman's Bible Commentary,* Vol. 22 (Richmond, Va.: John Knox Press, 1959), 72.

mutual subordination to what alone can nurture and deepen these commitments — a "reverence for Christ," a reverence for that illuminating and life-giving power that the *logos* brings into "flesh." Even after the "subjection" clause is introduced, the author avoids any and all talk of further subjugations, rankings, or divinely sanctioned natural orders. There are no grounds for a "dominator-marriage" in this text. Love, respect, tenderness, and commitment are the virtues that the Pauline writer extols.

As married couples know, no successful marriage is founded on "equalitarian" principles alone. Good marriages are founded on that Pauline understanding of love that "bears all things, believes all things, hopes all things, endures all things" (1 Cor. 13:7). That is the disposition that the author of Ephesians exalts. An attitude toward one's beloved that is never "arrogant," "boastful," or "rude," that avoids "insisting on its own way," and desires only what is best for the beloved. This attitude requires more than "equalitarianism." It requires commitment, intimacy, tenderness, sacrifice, the resolve that, by God's gracious help, this marriage will prevail. It invites humility and candor, the willingness to listen, to share, even one's deepest fears and deepest needs, and to embrace the other in the saddest of pains, for God has blessed it with a power to issue in a bonding that neither tears nor tragedy can sunder. It is worth every ounce of love and hope that two souls can give each other.

Marriage, as the author alludes, is a "mystery." It is a mystery of God's covenant with the elect, witnessing to the pledge that God made with Abraham, by whom "all the *families* of the earth shall be blessed" (NRSV Gen. 12:3 — italics for emphasis).

The General Epistles

Most scholars assign these letters to the last quarter of the first century, if not later, setting them in a time after the death of the apostles and the martyrdom of Paul. It was a period fraught with persecution, the rise of gnosticism and other heretical movements, and a time in the life of the church when its leaders sought to codify and traditionalize the faith. If in general this is true, what are the "virtues" that characterize the faith of this period and continue to possess validity for the Christian life?

Hebrews

Among the many themes developed in the Letter to the Hebrews, two are notable.

1. *Faith (pistis).* "For whoever would draw near to God must believe that he exists" (Heb. 11:6). Traditional Christianity, following Paul, has listed faith, hope, and love as the cardinal theological virtues. So too does the author of this letter, emphasizing hope as an aspect of faith (Heb. 11:1) and urging his readers to continue their ethic of love and hospitality (13:2).

The virtue of faith has repeatedly surfaced as a central value throughout this study. In particular, the Hebrew emphasis has consistently fallen on the virtue's *stabilizing* and *foundational* value. It is the *sine qua non* of the Christian life, second only to love.

Because the modern age has assigned importance to an epistemology that comprehends truth as something whose claims correspond to "empirical facts," it has been loathe to recognize the truth claims of traditional religious faith whose doctrines cannot be verified empirically. Modern rationalist epistemology reveals its own philosophical prejudice, its "empirical bias," making itself suspect.

Biblical and traditional concepts of Christian faith have long emphasized three factors: faith as a subjective response to the self-revelation of God (the Abrahamic via Kierkegaardian analysis), faith as an intelligent and moral response to the objective events of history (from Abraham through the apostles), and faith as a gift of God's gracious will for the human heart to entrust itself to the Divine. In each instance, "choice" is unavoidable and a requirement of every believer, though the members of the believing fellowship can be of great comfort.

Existentialist philosophers emphasize that human destiny is determined by one's choices. What persons do or fail to do, accept or fail to accept, become or fail to become is a matter of personal responsibility and freedom of choice. And it leads to either an "authentic" or an "inauthentic" existence. So too the Christian faith challenges believers to become authentic, to seek "authenticity," by taking responsibility for their own choices, actions, and values.

Faith, as a positive response to God's summons, is a critical virtue because it reminds believers that their myriad and inescapable choices mold and determine their total beingness, even within communities. Such is one's glory and fate as a human being created in the image of God. Every temptation to escape choice is doomed to fail; correspondingly, every temptation to avoid faith is, in itself, a form of bad faith.

God solicits faith, woos faith, seeks faith, engenders faith. God longs for all to become those authentic beings, whom the Divine has endowed with incredible gifts for moral and personal development, to live and grow in reciprocity with the Godhead and with neighbor.

Faith, as existential choice, becomes a principal determiner, molding the dispositions and actions persons elect to follow, and impinges on their life, even within the context of the household of faith. "For whoever would draw near to God must believe that he exists and that he rewards those who seek him" (Heb. 11:6).

2. *The Eternal Perspective.* Once again Christians are reminded of the mystery that the moral life is inextricably bound up with the principle of *sub specie aeternitatis.* Though theologically in agreement with Paul, the author of the Letter to the Hebrews expresses the theme uniquely:

> These all died in faith, not having received what was promised, but having seen it and greeted it from afar, and having acknowledged that they were strangers and exiles on the earth. . . . But as it is, they desire a better country. . . . Therefore God . . . has prepared for them a city. (Heb. 11:13-16)

> And all these . . . did not receive what was promised, since God had foreseen something better for us, that apart from us they should not be made perfect. (Heb. 11:39-40)

This side of eternity, any moral agent whose faith is rooted in Christ will experience "exile." She or he will know herself or himself to be a "stranger," whose value system will always fall shy of the world's full approval. Indeed, it will fall shy of one's own ultimate satisfaction. But this is owing to the fact that this side of eternity is but a fragment of God's "time," of God's hope and "vision" of the whole, which God sees perfectly from the divine side of eternity.

Therefore, one may "lay aside every weight" and anxiety that would distract one and "run with perseverance the race that is set before us, looking to Jesus the pioneer and perfecter of our faith" (Heb. 12:1-2).

James

Many of James' virtues echo Paul's. Unlike Paul's, however, each is set within the context of a homily. They resemble moral exhortations, but still they express theological virtues. On the whole, they call Christians to *steadfastness, industry,* and *hope.* Besides these he lists: *wisdom, endurance, works, impartiality, restraint of the tongue, humility, patience,* and *confession.*

Luther considered this letter a "strawy epistle," but three of James' "virtues" attract attention.

1. *Wisdom (sophia).* "If any of you lacks wisdom, let him ask God, who gives to all men generously and without reproaching, and it will be given him" (Jas. 1:5).

What is the *sophia* that Christians require in order to discover authentic life, becoming what God has created them to be? In retrospect, is it not the wisdom to love the Eternal God with all one's heart, mind, and soul and one's neighbor as oneself? Is it not the wisdom to live all one's life *coram Deo,* "in the presence of God," preferring God's will, kingdom, and ordering of what leads to the best, to one's own? Is it not the wisdom of acknowledging that although, at the present, one sees "through the glass darkly," from God's side of eternity all is well? Does it not incorporate the wisdom that "God was in Christ," the eternal *logos,* "reconciling the world to himself," so that everything which had heretofore *"bound"* humans has now been swept aside? So that they are now "free" to use all their God-endowed potential for the glory of God and good of neighbor? Is this not the *sophia* that constitutes the Christian's highest good and eventuates in each believer's highest satisfaction?

2. *Works (erga)*. Works are products of action; they are deeds resulting from a deliberate course of pursuit. That is what the Greek word means. Luther did not like this "virtue," because he feared it would undo salvation by grace through faith and rekindle the vain delusions of works-righteousness. His warning has merit. Yet, James's exhortation to *erga* is not without value. For *works* are the true actions that flow out of faith. Writes James: "faith by itself, if it has no works, is dead" (Jas. 2:17).

From a universal standpoint, Aristotle would concur. So would Aquinas. Being and action are one. For both Aquinas and Aristotle, "virtuous activity," or its absence, defines human beings as much as "contemplation." The highest happiness consists in both action and thought. Thus moral acts which shape character reveal thought as much as they contribute to the advancement of good, for self or neighbor. Actions witness to faith and to the saving reality of God who calls all to exercise "love, joy, peace," and the other virtues. Hence, their absence should concern the Christian community, not because their presence guarantees salvation, as James seems to imply — which is why Luther objected — but because their absence raises the possibility that the believer may still be committed to self rather than to God, that he or she may still be bound to the self and thus bound to forfeit the wholeness that God longs for him or her to know.

It is of interest to note that the biblical ethicist T. B. Maston defends James' call to works. Maston argues that James was not concerned with "the works of the Law" but only with "good deeds in general." Maston explains: "The primary concern of James is with sanctification and not justification. Progress in the former is evidence of the latter. In other words, for James the only kind of faith that saves or justifies is a faith that is meaningful enough to produce . . . good deeds."[7]

3. *Confession*. The Greek verb is *exomologeo*. "Confess your sins to one another, and pray for one another, that you may be

7. Maston, *Biblical Ethics*, 263-64.

healed" (Jas. 5:16). The need for confession applies here to both the individual and the community. It is inseparable from true healing. Indeed, what is this "healing" to which James alludes? Is it not the realization that, this side of eternity, Christians stand in constant need of each other and in need of each other's forgiveness, and, therefore, in need of repentance and of each other's forbearance?

In the final analysis, forgiveness, confession, and repentance are vital to a Christian moral life. *Semper iustus et peccator.* The fact that this is true is not meant to discourage, but to encourage the believer. For confession, repentance, and forgiveness not only suggest how one might act toward one's neighbor but also depict the depth of one's own need before God.

Peter's Letters

More so than the Letter to the Hebrews or James' Epistle, Peter's correspondence witnesses to that intensely held first-century belief in the imminence of Christ's return. It dominated Paul's thought and Peter's as well. "The end of all things is at hand" (1 Pet. 4:7). Consequently, Peter's letters emphasize a high degree of submissiveness to the constructive orders that exist (the state and the family), and a need to attain to a "sobriety" appropriate to the "last days." He calls on all to trust God, as never before, casting all their anxiety on the Divine.

1. *Submissiveness.* "Be subject . . . to every human institution" (1 Pet. 2:13). The verb, *Hypotasso,* rendered "be subject" in English, means to bring oneself *under the influence of.* The Greek noun, *ktisis,* refers to a created institution. Peter knows that there are created human institutions that exist as phenomena of God's will and that have sprung out of the human quest for solid universal principles. He will not debase this ethical dimension of God's ordering for humankind's highest good, even if it is a good created out of the *human* quest for wholeness. Nor should we debase it. Wherever there are sound ethical and universal institutions and principles at work, to that extent God's mind and will for humankind are being witnessed to. Rather than attacking them, the Christian is encouraged to support them and welcome them as "tools of God's

love," to use Tolstoy's phrase. Of course, this does not mean supporting oppressive economic or political systems, though it may mean enduring unjust programs while one works toward the collective good, since "governors [are] sent by him to punish those who do wrong and to praise those who do right" (1 Pet. 2:14). The whole gamut of citizenship falls within the purview of a Christian's commitment to God and neighbor. Certainly, Calvin understood it in this manner and gave it eloquent and pragmatic expression in his theology of the Christian magistrate. In short, the Christian community ought to care about magisterial institutions.

Peter's "submissiveness," however, is not a call to "passivity." It is rather a call to a form of political and moral sensitivity, worthy of a Christian's commitment to God's "best-ordering" ideal. Peter writes: "Conduct yourselves honorably among the Gentiles, . . . that by doing right you should silence the ignorance of the foolish," living "as free people," yet not using "your freedom as a pretext for evil" (NRSV 1 Pet. 2:12, 15-16). Here is an active commitment to the best that the ethical and the universal can provide for the good of all human beings. Even in the worst of circumstances Peter calls upon Christians to exercise the maximum peace and love they are capable of, in order to influence the political orders of their time. It is a response of respect for all just systems of due-process while ever caring about miscarriages of justice. For this reason the Christian is to "Maintain good conduct among the Gentiles so that . . . they may see your good deeds and glorify God" (1 Pet. 2:12). A Christian, in service to God, will engage in the realm of the ethical and the universal, the political and the communal, precisely in obedience to God and in service to Christ Jesus, who is "the way and the truth and the life."

In his own analysis of this Petrine virtue, R. E. O. White observes that "the catechetical theme of submission to just authority" is "the pre-eminent concept"; and so the proper frame for all piety is "humility under the mighty hand of God." Thus, "subordination elaborated as a social code is simply the application to daily life of this . . . virtue of reverence."[8]

8. R. E. O. White, *Biblical Ethics* (Atlanta: John Knox Press, 1979), 188-89.

2. *Sobriety.* Once again the New Testament confronts the believer with the verb *sophroneo,* to be sober-minded, sedate, sane. Commitment to the ethical requires "sobriety." "Keep sane and sober"; "be prepared to make a defense"; "keep your conscience clear"; be prepared to be "abused" (1 Pet. 3–4 passim). Sobriety is a virtue insofar as it enables one to become alert to what is going on. Gullibility is not a virtue, neither at the universal nor Christian level. Someone unalert and easily duped can be of service neither to God nor neighbor, especially to the latter in a time of crisis or need. The "sobriety" involved is a call for more than "temperance." The brunt of this Petrine virtue is for every Christian to be sensibly tough-minded, astutely aware, and spiritually savvy to be of maximum usefulness to Christ, community, and neighbor. Sobriety too is integral to a *theologia crucis.*

3. *Trust.* Finally, Peter emphasizes "trust," or entrusting one's entire well-being to God. "Humble yourselves therefore under the mighty hand of God, that in due time he may exalt you. Cast all your anxieties on him, for he cares for you" (1 Pet. 5:6-7). The call to *tapeinoo* is a call to be "humble with respect to hope." For Peter, there is no shame in humility before God, in recognizing one's anxieties, or in casting them on God. The Christian life, like Aristotle's summer day, does not consist in a single swallow's flight. Again, it is a process, requiring renewal, forgiveness, continued growth in grace, and the nurturing support of both the Spirit and the community of believers. For this reason, God invites us to trust the Divine and to bring every anxious and ambivalent reservation to God's presence. As the waiting father in the Parable of the Prodigal Son, daily anticipated his son's return, so God awaits those private times one spends with the Divine. "For he cares for you," Peter writes.

The Johannine Correspondence

John's letters also reflect the lateness of the hour and the belief in Christ's imminent return. It is "the last hour," and the stage is set for the "antichrist" (1 John 2:18). For the most part, the virtues required here are similar to those of the Gospel of John, with special emphasis on "abiding in Christ" and the need to demonstrate the "love commandment." However, John does list additional virtues.

1. *Maintaining a Relative Relationship to the Relative.* "Do not love the world or the things in the world," for all that panders to the "lust of the flesh and the lust of the eyes and the pride of life . . . passes away" (1 John 2:15-17). Only one reality seeks, deserves, and requires the believer's absolute and ultimate relationship. Everything else remains relative even if urgent. That one reality is God and God alone. "For those who want to save their life will lose it, and those who lose their life for my sake will find it" (NRSV Matt. 16:25).

In all ages, humankind is lulled into allowing the humanly urgent and relative to usurp a higher loyalty than the heart knows it should. The "pride of life" and "the lust of the eyes" distract the self. They promise so much, but in the end undermine and erode the self that God has created each human being capable of becoming.

John reminds his readers of the crucial stance the believer must take if one's fullness of humanity is to be realized. What John asks of the Christian is nothing less than what God asked of Abraham and the saints of old: an absolute devotion to the Eternal. It is the principle of God first and foremost, God's will and kingdom made primary. Then everything else will ensue as it should. As Augustine himself put it: "Love God and do as you will."[9]

2. *Discernment.* "Beloved, do not believe every spirit, but test the spirits to see whether they are of God" (1 John 4:1). As gullibility is unacceptable in the moral and ethical arena, so is it detrimental at the theological and philosophical level. The true moral agent must ever submit her own moral and philosophical assumptions, and those of her age, to criticism. How well does any system of belief, lifestyle, worldview, or ethical parameter measure up against God's truth, as incarnated in the Eternal *logos*

---

9. See Augustine's *Epistle of St. John*, Homily VII, 8; *On Nature and Grace*, LXX (84); and *On Christian Doctrine*, I, 28 (42); cited by T. J. Bigham and A. T. Mollegen in Ch. XIV, "The Christian Ethic," in Roy W. Battenhouse's *A Companion to the study of St. Augustine* (New York: Oxford University Press, 1955), 377.

of Christ? How does it compare when juxtaposed against that world of grace spelled out so explicitly in Scripture?

The same must be asked of the community's theological views as well. To what extent do they actually witness to *sola Deo* and *sola scriptura?* Or do they represent compromises that preserve a sanctuary for the self or postpone the healing encounter with the sole Reality that can save and fulfill, both morally and spiritually?

The Christian is called upon to exercise *discernment.* Jesus says, "Be wise as serpents and innocent as doves" (Matt. 10:16). He said this to his disciples as he sent them out for the first time. "Behold, I send you out as sheep in the midst of wolves" (Matt. 10:16).

Discernment is a Christian virtue, because it reminds believers of the subtleties that can and do erode the Christian life. It reminds each Christian of his or her need to hold to God first, to long for God's will to prevail, to be willing to set self aside, to be savvy, alert and aware and always open to "good" as God would define it, whatever the situation, whatever the hour. For John, there can be no substitute for this kind of discernment. Great peace comes in exercising it faithfully.

3. *Reaffirming the Faith.* John concludes by calling upon the Christian community to reaffirm the centrality of Christ and by warning the faithful against "idols." What alone can keep the Christian in the way of truth and human wholeness? John answers:

> By this you know the Spirit of God: every spirit which confesses that Jesus Christ has come in the flesh is of God. . . . And we know that the Son of God has come and has given us understanding, to know him who is true; and we are in him who is true, in his Son Jesus Christ. . . . Little children, keep yourselves from idols. (1 John 4:2; 5:20-21)

The modern age spawns doubt, doubt as to the reality of an absolute principle of moral significance, as well as doubt in an absolute being of moral essence and character. In stead of either, it proffers a closed system, or naturalistic order, wonderful and awesome to be sure, but nonetheless encapsulated within its own mysterious principles and cycles and uncertain fate. In this system, who one is and what one does are purely relative to time and culture, or to the cycles of nature, and ultimately have no final bearing on, or relevance, to the beginning or end of the cosmos, time, nature, or history.

But in the Christian tradition, the Eternal God, who meets all humankind in the Bible, both calls us to long for more by questioning us as to the very nature of our being. "What is man that thou art mindful of him?" is a universal question, which every age has been summoned to raise. The *question* may be answered differently by different cultures at different times in different ages, but the question is one and the same and ultimately inescapable.

John reminds Christians that the Eternal God, as the *logos,* from the beginning nudged the souls of those first true human beings (the biblical Adam and Eve) to respond to God, and thus began that unique history of self-revelation with Abraham and his posterity. We are reminded too that God has revealed the divine fullness in Jesus Christ and continues by the power of the Holy Spirit to confirm and fulfill this truth in every heart that responds to God. When Jesus says "I am the way and the truth and the life," "he who loses his life for my sake will find it," he is himself confirming what the entire Hebrew Bible declares: that God has created human beings in the divine image and endowed them with incredible potential for moral growth and good, creating them for a reciprocity with the Divine and neighbor which truly enables each human being to become all that God longs for him or her to experience. But shy of a reciprocity founded on love for God and love for neighbor, humankind will always fall short of the highest development God has willed that each should attain.

This truth of human wholeness has been witnessed to not only by Scripture but, in the modern era, by philosophers as well. Few have put it as powerfully as Gabriel Marcel — the late, French, theistic existentialist. Writes Marcel:

> A man cannot be free or remain free, except in the degree to which he remains linked with that which transcends him. . . . When I myself speak here of a recourse to the transcendent, I mean . . . a level of being, an order of the spirit, which is also the level and order of grace, of mercy, of charity; and to proclaim . . . that we do not belong entirely to the world of objects to which men are seeking to assimilate us, in which they are strain-

ing to imprison us. . . . [Rather] we have to proclaim that this life of ours . . . may in reality be only the most insignificant aspect of a grand process unfolding itself far beyond the boundaries of the visible world.[10]

10. Gabriel Marcel, *Man Against Mass Society,* cited by Robert C. Solomon in *Existentialism* (New York: Modern Library, 1974), 131.

CHAPTER SIX

Virtue and the Christian Life: A Final Assessment

A RECURRING THEME in this exploration has been the biblical emphasis that the Creator of the universe has fashioned humankind in the image of God and has endowed each man and woman with incredible potential for moral and intellectual development as well as for intimate and relational commitments. God has done so for the primary purpose of human wholeness in reciprocity with the Divine and neighbor. For the Christian, authentic wholeness incorporates this profound belonging to God and steadfast commitment to neighbor.

This conviction does not preclude the belief that God has created human beings as distinct individuals. A whole line of philosophical theology is devoted to defending such uniqueness under the rubric of "secondary causes" and their proper, self-perpetuating, and self-accountable quality. But, as Jesus explains, "those who want to save their life will lose it, and those who lose their life for my sake, and for the sake of the gospel, will save it" (NRSV Mark 8:35). For the Christian community, the essential meaning of human existence lies in this paradox. Though God has created humankind as unique individuals, each comes to fruition only to the extent that he or she surrenders himself or herself to the Eternal and opens the self to one's neighbor in love.

In the Christian faith, the eternal God of the universe has

always sought out humankind first, extending unmerited grace to all. It is God's grace and initiative that are the foundation of the human response and make it possible. Thus in Christian theology justification by grace through faith is prior to sanctification. This means nothing less than a Christian's highest good. For it means that believers are free from the curse of every impossible and vain attempt to justify the self. They are liberated from becoming what they cannot become on their own and are freed to grow toward becoming the persons God desires them to be.

The preceding chapters have sought to identify the biblical virtues that flow from and shape Christian character. Based, then, upon biblical principles, virtue may be defined as *an activity of the whole person in conformity with love of God and love of neighbor.* Such virtue is subordinate to a way of life that surrenders its orientation to God. That being true, the virtues become those positive responses that enable one to experience and exercise love of God and love of neighbor. The extent to which one actualizes this love is the extent to which one *becomes* what God longs for one to be. Finally, this study has emphasized the relational and communal context in which the unfolding of this process occurs.

It is important now to reflect on three interrelated areas: (1) the virtues and their significance for the self; (2) the virtues and their impact on others, and (3) the virtues and their relevance for a pluralistic age.

The Self-Regarding Virtues and the Christian Life

Philosophers and ethicists make a distinction between "self-regarding" virtues and "other-regarding" virtues. Self-regarding virtues refer to those dispositions and actions that both flow from and deepen a person's moral development or contribute to an individual's own moral good. Other-regarding virtues have to do with attitudes and actions that impact on other persons. In each instance, the virtues possess and exercise "instrumental value" in shaping the self and society as well as in reinforcing the soundness of character in which they are embodied.

Because of the nature of the Christian life and its specific orientation toward God, the instrumental value of the self-regarding virtues and their significance for the molding of the self make them of special interest to the present exploration. In what sense are the "self-regarding" virtues relevant to the Christian life? Or do they detract from it? Can the so-called "self-regarding" virtues exercise any true normative role in "shaping" the Christian life? Are they not already dependent upon and subordinate to one's response to God? Is not all talk about the virtues in fact superfluous if not in opposition to Jesus' dictum that whoever seeks to save his or her life will lose it?

If this study has educed any clear general principles at all, it should be clear from those principles that the answer to the last question must be "No." In both the Old and the New Testaments, when believers yield willingly to God, then the power and Spirit of God lead them into lifestyles that more fittingly witness to their orientation in the Eternal and which, in the process, deepen their sense of wholeness as human beings. To that extent, the consequent dispositions that emerge, along with the moral habits one establishes, have significant instrumental value in shaping a believer's life and its impact on others.

In no instance, however, does this "influencing" or "shaping" make one "better" or "superior" in the eyes of God. It is God's loving and electing initiative alone that constitutes the believer's "specialness" in both Testaments. But the ways in which believers respond do influence their unique, particular, and individual realizations of God's love. The Christian *new being* that emerges in surrender to God is enriched by the attitudes and dispositions that both Testaments extol. In that way the biblical virtues are greatly instrumental in reinforcing the moral character that is hidden in God. As Hauerwas suggests, the quality of life a Christian enjoys is inseparable from this interplay of character and virtue.

From that biblical perspective, a reexamination of the self-regarding virtues is important.

1. Freedom, Self-Accountability, and God. Faith is the virtue, along with love, that most opens Christians to moral soundness. As a virtue it is inseparable from freedom and self-accountability.

Freedom means that human beings are accountable for what

they do and for what happens to them. Freedom and accountability are the twin dynamics that underlie faith; they constitute faith's foundation. But because of the radical consequences of the Fall, the Bible (especially Paul) understands the extent to which these foundations have been brought into question. "For I do not do the good I want, but the evil I do not want is what I do" (Rom. 7:19). If it were not for the fact that God acts first, comes and stirs hearts to respond to the Divine, no one would be free to rise above the pride, guilt, diffuseness, and inauthenticity that characterize the human condition. Without God's grace, without God's forgiveness of pride and loss of self-wholeness, acts of freedom and account-ability would remain bound by a darkness of the self — a darkness whose levels even of goodness would be overshadowed by the constant presence of inauthenticity. Even as the redeemed children of God, the residue of this inauthenticity lives on in believers.

In the same way that God's free electing initiative in the Hebrew Bible provides the foundation for ancient Israel's response, so Christ's life, death, and resurrection in the New Testament provides the foundation for the Christian response. Liberated from the curse of the self's pride and guilt, or from the loss of a central focus and abandonment to triviality, Christ's disciples are free to respond to God as selves *simul et semper iustus et peccator,* but nonetheless as selves free to account for their lives in radically new ways. Each is liberated to discover the deepest dimensions of one's wholeness, sexuality, and unique beingness. However, this is still one's own decision to make, even though the possibility of making it is a gift of God.

Christians can never escape this freedom. God longs for each to use it to say "Yes" to the Divine. But no one is obligated to do so. Even a person's No falls within the framework of God's will. The Reformed rubric of "irresistible grace" is not without merit here, for biblical salvation is always a gift. Humans are never the principal agents of their redemption. God remains the final determiner of the mystery of salvation. Nevertheless, whatever the response, no one can escape this freedom. And to that extent, within the mystery of the divine concurrence, a person's response shapes his life, deter-mines the degree to which he or she is free from the past, as well as how open an individual's present and future might be.

Within the boundaries of God's concurring will, what a Christian does and what happens to him or her is inescapably his or her own doing. Everyone is accountable. It is the biblical way of attesting to the *minor gloria creaturae,* while equally affirming the *maior Dei gloria.* God's hope is that all will believe and will entrust themselves to the Eternal, so that the new self that emerges will experience its full potential as a living and moral entity in God, and as a unique member of the body of Christ.

Since it is by the mystery of grace that one's "Yes" or "No" molds one's destiny, *faith* is a paramount virtue. What a person believes and values, what he or she dares to become and be, or what communities and relationships he or she wills to support and cherish, have tremendous impact on shaping character. They have the power to unleash or repress potential, as well as control and direct future possibilities. As humans project themselves into the future, how they respond to God's grace will either enlarge or fossilize their being. The good news of Christianity is that the self that surrenders to God is the self that paradoxically finds its wholeness. Correspondingly, the self that remains within itself is a self that can never rise above the limitations of its fragmented beingness.

As Marcel has put it so ably, human life "diminishes in proportion as the soul becomes increasingly chained to its experiences."[1] But in contrast to this "captive soul," the person whose being "is at the disposal of others," and ultimately at the disposal of God, is "protected against despair," because such a soul "knows that it is not its own, and that the most legitimate use it can make of its freedom is precisely to recognize that it does not belong to itself."[2] For Marcel, this "recognition" is the true starting point of all genuine human "activity and creativeness."

Hence, faith as a self-regarding virtue is instrumental in determining the kind of self one becomes. It either advances the new being God has made possible for one to attain, or results in one's forfeiting what beingness one has.

---

1. Marcel, *The Philosophy of Existentialism,* trans. Manya Harari (Sylvancus, N.J.: The Citadel Press, 1973), 43.
2. Ibid.

2. Discernment, Wisdom, Repentance. Equally important as faith are the concomitant virtues of discernment, wisdom, and repentance. One might also add here the principle of *sub specie aeternitatis*.

From the human side of time, the future can never be known except "in part"; one can never see it except "in a mirror dimly." Of necessity, persons are forced to anticipate it; they cannot help but project themselves into it. That is what it means to be a person whose humanness occurs in time. No one can escape time, no more than choice, for time too defines human beings. All of us, by virtue of our humanness, cannot help but transcend present time and, by projecting ourselves into the future, wonder what else we might become or fail to become.

For the Christian, neither this condition of human existence nor time itself is an enemy. One does not have to fear time, though the present may be filled with anxiety, moments of ambiguity, and tension, and the future fraught with uncertainty. Such is the nature of finitude, which God created and pronounced "good."

Rather, what the *euangelion* of the Christian faith proclaims is that the Creator-God of the universe, whom it has come to know in the Hebrew Bible and in the Divine self-revelation in Christ, is the God of time. The Creator-God alone can truly fulfill destinies for human beings and moral creatures. Hence the *euangelion* calls upon the believing community, willfully and wisely, to acknowledge and obey this sole Creator-God as the primary illuminating and highest ordering goodness in one's life.

It is the acceptance of this good news that constitutes the Christian's *wisdom* that issues in a believer's highest joy. As Paul writes:

> Among the mature we do impart wisdom, although it is not a wisdom of this age or of the rulers of this age, who are doomed to pass away. But we impart a secret and hidden wisdom of God, which God decreed before the ages for our glorification. (1 Cor. 2:6-7)

Remaining faithful to this wisdom, recommitting oneself to it as humankind's only and highest hope, and allowing God's will and desired ordering of life to establish the highest criteria for one's own discernments of good and evil is what keeps life human. It is God's wisdom that constitutes the Christian's "glory" as a being created in the divine image, fashioned for membership in the family of faith. And it is this wisdom, from God's side of time, that will prevail and render one's life and Christ's *ekklesia* meaningful.

3. Joy, Peace, Equanimity, Power. Because of what God has done in Christ, true joy and peace are accessible; they can be experienced by the community of faith. Abraham, Joseph, Gideon, Hannah, Bathsheba, all came to experience that peace and power that faith in God alone inspires. It is the peace and equanimity that Jesus extols, indeed promises to his believers, which his paradigmatic servants, maidens, and wise stewards so compelling mirror. It is the same peace that Paul calls all to claim as a gift of the Holy Spirit. And though Christians possess it as a treasure in an earthen vessel, still it is theirs to claim and to have.

Joy. Peace. Equanimity. Power. They flow from God's assurance that one belongs to the Eternal. That nothing can separate one from God. Neither death nor dying, ambiguity nor insecurity, nothing can separate the disciple from God's love in Christ Jesus. All belong to God. Not even the threat of anonymity, sin, triviality, or physical annihilation can have the last word. It is God alone, who, from the aspect of eternity, will pronounce the final, definitive word that where Christ is there will his disciples be also.

Again as Marcel has eloquently phrased it: "My life infinitely transcends my possible conscious grasp of my life at any given moment; fundamentally and essentially it refuses to tally with itself."[3] Or again, "The question, 'What is my worth?' is an insoluble riddle. It can only become an appeal to the Absolute Thou."[4] Or as a character in my story *"The Demoniac,"* puts it to a wretched man living in the drains of a city: "Whoever you are, whatever you've done, whatever's been done to you, . . . you are infinitely more than the worst that has happened to you."[5]

---

3. Marcel, *The Mystery of Being,* Vol. I, *Reflections & Mystery* (Chicago: Henry Regnery Co., 1950), 167.

4. Ibid., 154.

5. See Benjamin W. Farley, *Cry of the Hawk.* Forthcoming.

The good news of the Christian faith is that God's love justifies every human life. No soul, no one's existence or beingness is superfluous. Which is why all need the voice of their fellow Christian, their sister believer, whenever one's own hope is low.

4. Courage, Sobriety, and Self-Control. But now, on this side of eternity, the joy of becoming what God wills for the believer to be is no small task. Courage, sobriety, and self-control have immense instrumental value for assisting one in the process. Everyone needs them, both to exercise and embody them. In God's eyes, they cannot make one better, but they can and do contribute to the depth of one's wholeness as a person whose hopes lie in God and whose joy comes in sharing life with others. Hence, to that end, self-indulgence, moral weakness, and cowardice detract from the depth and breadth of one's Christian "becoming." They limit one's potential as a being who, created in God's image, has been so fashioned that the full blossoming of one's humanness is impossible aside from a person's commitments to others and his or her willingness to transcend the self, which requires courage, sobriety, and self-control. One cannot be "whole" without them, though their absence has never deterred God from loving any believer. But, again, they too are "gifts" of God's Spirit, gifts that God wants and longs for all to claim. "Take them," God urges. "Be strong. Come; deny yourself; take up your cross and follow me. For whoever loses his life for my sake and the gospel's will find it."

From a biblical point of view, there is no shame in a Christian claiming these virtues, as long as he or she remembers to whom one belongs and clings to God as one's Redeemer.

Other-Regarding Virtues and the Christian Life

It is of interest to note that in Aristotle's catalog of twelve virtues, only two (truthfulness and justice) are decidedly "other-regarding" or "outward-directed," though eight of the remaining (generosity, magnanimity, high-mindedness, gentleness, pleasantness, friendliness, modesty, and righteous indignation) clearly impact on others. This is understandable. A glance at these last eight indicates that

Aristotle's primary goal was to advance the self's highest happiness, not humankind's or a community's in general, though the latter was of keen interest to him, and he was frequently called upon to write constitutions for neighboring city-states. In fact, in his *Politics,* he argues that the state takes precedence over the individual, as the individual needs the state to attain life's higher satisfactions. But this never curtails his interest in urging individuals to become as virtuous as their natures allow.

In contrast, the biblical emphasis on neighbor vis-à-vis the self is unremitting. For the state should never take precedence over individuals or their collective unity, since the state is not life's highest end. Nonetheless, one's neighbor is a central phenomenological aspect of one's beingness, if not an ontological aspect of one's beingness, and is to be loved as much as the self. For, phenomenologically, the neighbor has also been created in the image of God and, ontologically, has been created out of the same essence as the self (male and female in the Priestly account, out of "dust" and "rib" in the Yahwist account) precisely because God understands that humanness devoid of intimate social reciprocity is not a suitable condition for mankind. In the Genesis 1:26 passage, "male and female" are created simultaneously; while in the Genesis 2:18 story, God declares that it is "not good for man to be alone."

With that as a preamble, there are two central features that command attention for the Christian. The first has to do with the universal quality which characterizes the other-regarding virtues; the second has to do with Christianity's unique contribution to and potential significance for those virtues.

1. The Universal Quality of the Other-Regarding Virtues. In his book, *The Right and the Good,* W. D. Ross identifies six *prima facie* duties which rational minds are capable of discovering. The six are his way of analyzing the Eternal law of God that mankind's unaided reason is able to grasp — although he does not designate their source as the Eternal Law of God. Earlier in this study we were introduced to "fidelity." Ross identifies the remaining five as: gratitude, justice, beneficence, self-improvement, and noninjury.[6]

6. W. D. Ross, *The Right and the Good* (Oxford: Clarendon Press, 1930), 19ff.

Clearly five of these are "other-regarding" virtues and parallel corresponding virtues extolled in both the Hebrew Bible and the New Testament.

Throughout this study, we have acknowledged the ethical and the universal dimensions that characterize the Bible's approved moral dispositions. And we have observed that this dimension poses no problem for either Christian theology or Christian practice. On the contrary, as we have shown, the Bible witnesses to the universal virtues of justice, fidelity, gratitude, respect, truthfulness, honesty, mercy, and kindness as God's way of uniting all human beings with one another that they might experience as much reciprocity with each other as possible.

For this reason, the other-regarding virtues are of great value, as they constantly remind the Christian that he lives for "ends" far higher than his own and for a brotherhood and sisterhood that transcend his own personal, social, or religious preferences. Consequently, the realm of the ethical and the universal, the relational and the communal, is not to be deprecated by Christians; it forms their link with fellow-humanity, whatever one's culture, politics, ethics, or religion.

Christians, therefore, demonstrate their love of God and love for neighbor wherever and whenever they embrace gratitude, justice, fidelity, truthfulness, beneficence, noninjury, and kindness. These duties constitute the willed virtues God requires all to honor and practice toward one's neighbor. Hence, as Peter urgently reminds us, Christians ought to care about the institutions that humanize their common adventure as God's children. With the Decalogue, the Covenant Code, the prophets, and Jesus' paradigmatic figures, we are to comfort and care for the hungry, thirsty, displaced, imprisoned, sick, and exiled. For God has "made from one every nation of men" (Acts 17:26). We are, therefore, our "brother's keeper."

Even Nietzsche understands this and, in his inimitable and inimical way, longed to see a Europe that would rise out of the ashes of its "slave morality" of "vengeance" and "spite" to recover a bold new ethics of what is "good" and "noble." So too Christians are called to be committed to what is good and noble in behalf of all.

2. Christianity's Significance for the Other-Regarding Virtues.

The compelling universal and ethical quality of the other-regarding virtues, however, constitutes but one side of the Christian call to love one's neighbor. For the Christian is called to love the neighbor *in a way* that transcends what the universal alone requires. The Christian is to love the neighbor as one loves oneself and to love one's neighbor as God in Christ loves the believer. Two things, then, clearly emerge that go beyond what the universal requires: (a) commitments to *ends* that transcend the highest conceived by the universal and (b) submission to a *grace* that transforms the heart and even the ethical and the universal themselves.

Aristotle identifies happiness as the highest end toward which humanity can move. To attain it, a life lived in conformity with reason is required. A life of reason, in turn, summons the rational soul to steer a course midway between excess and deficiency. When so pursued, then one will do the right thing at the right time in the right way for the right reason and experience satisfaction in doing so.

But the Bible understands something that has gone askew in humanity that Aristotle's era, though he sensed it, was unable to articulate in any satisfactory manner. That is, that the human will, in choosing its ends, is bound to choose ends that are self-inclined and characterized by an inordinate pride in conflict with itself or by a self that has forfeited its authentic beingness due to its own inertia and diffuseness. The self, in bondage to itself, can never rise above the ambivalence and insecurity that marks its existence. Even its acts of "freedom" are therefore less free than it supposes, and without forgiveness, it can never be free to attain the dimensions of humanness that God longs for humanity to know.

On earth and in society one may be able to attain an imperfect happiness, but as Aquinas admitted it can never substitute for the perfect happiness that God wants all believers to experience. From the Christian viewpoint, even this imperfect happiness turns out to be quite less "happy" than humans want, for it will degenerate to that level of culture that even Nietzsche faults and rejects because of its ethic of vengeance, spite, and its spirit of "nausea."

It is the same level of culture that Augustine depicts in the *City of God* and which he calls the "City of Man," whose "ends," however noble, are nonetheless ends dominated by a love of self, gain, and power. However noble the human attempt to serve the ethical and the universal may be, it will always be marred by a spirit of pride or anxiety and abandonment.

Thus, in honoring the virtues of the ethical and the universal, the Christian understands that looming above them is the loving Creator-God of the universe, whose will for humankind far exceeds the highest good that submission to the universal can bestow. The Christian's *ends* are simply different.

The other quality of the Christian ethic that transcends the unviersal is *grace*. The Christian life includes a *grace* that deepens and strengthens the Christian pursuit of God's highest "ends" for humanity. For God in Christ has set each believer free and accompanies each by the power of the Holy Spirit to nurture and deepen the gifts of faith and love that make possible the attainment of God's desired goals. To that end, the Christian virtues of *faith, hope,* and *love* are instrumental, which each Christian has the joyful task of bringing to his or her exercise of the universal virtues.

In this light, let us consider each of the theological virtues, beginning with faith, which is instrumental for attaining the higher calling in at least four ways.

1. It witnesses to society at large that there are values and commitments that transcend the self and take precedence over an ethic of egoism, however ethically enlightened and subservient that egoism might be. It rightly acknowledges the uniqueness of the self, but it equally attests to the uniqueness and presence of others and the fact that one's life is but a single thread of a rich fabric of interrelationships. This is why membership in the household of faith can be so satisfying.

2. It witnesses to the truth that aside from forgiveness, mercy, and grace (Marcel's levels of transcendence) there can be no true human freedom. Aside from forgiveness, human beings are the inevitable prisoners of a self that knows that one could have chosen to act other than one did, but must now live with the remorse of one's choices and the hurt they cause others.

3. It offers a vision of the world that does justice to a principle of meaning and order at both the cosmic and historical level. It rejects both empiricism's materialistic bias and worldview as well as mysticism's contentment to be nurtured by nature. Rather, in the name of God's wonder and transcendence, faith invites and

challenges the human community to opt for a higher criterion of hope than a materialistic reductionism can provide. To that end, it knows that choice is unavoidable and that, in the final analysis, within the framework of God's providence, every individual is accountable for what he or she does, believes, and becomes. Thus it challenges all of us to reconsider the modern worldview and to accept God in the very name of the wonder and transcendence all humans experience.

4. Faith in God deepens one's sense of wholeness as a human being by keeping one open to the self-revealing God of Scripture and the reality, presence, and needs of one's neighbor. Consequently, in doing so it offers a context for responsible commitment at the level of the ethical and the universal and can lead to profound healing and new opportunities for self and neighbor.

Hope. Hope too is of equal merit, for it also possesses instrumental value. If faith provides the highest context for clarifying a moral agent's commitment to moral values, hope supplies the sustaining courage needed for perseverance and endurance.

In the same way that choice is unavoidable, so also is time. One cannot avoid anticipating the future. What Christian hope, based on its faith in God, is willing to risk is that the future one faces is filled with the reality, kindness, and the power of God. Now one sees in part; then one shall know as one is fully known. Christian hope understands that from this side of time one can never see more than in a mirror dimly. One can never escape one's finitude, sexuality, or particular ambiance of time and place. Nor does one need to. For, from God's side of time, God's purposes in Jesus Christ will prevail. God's love will have the last and definitive word. Therefore, from within this side of time, *sub specie aeternitatis,* one may act with courage, industry, joy, anticipation, faithfulness, boldness, and peace.

This means that the Christian virtue of hope brings more than perspective to the ethical scene. It does more than undergird the universal. It nurtures courage, bolsters determination, and invites involvement, commitment, fidelity, and caring. It especially fosters the latter, for since the Christian knows that he belongs to God and not to the self, his mind and heart are buoyed by that Eternal presence whose power is made perfect in weakness, thus providing the grace and wherewithal to surmount personal despair.

Furthermore, by exercising the virtue of hope, the Christian brings to the world a new vitality, a new daring for facing the future with courage, confidence, sanguiness. It enables the Christian to offer hope and encouragement, not merely to one's fellow believer, but to all one's neighbors.

The modern era tends toward despair. It is noted for its despair. In spite of its allegiance to the ethical and the universal, which provides a moral consensus, the modern era still evinces a form of quiet, jaded acquiescence that neither its sometime enlightened altruism nor its oftentimes tawdry Epicureanism can dispel. "Why not evince it?" the modern world asks. "What more is there to embrace?" To which Christianity responds, "The Eternal God. Because our very need to transcend ourselves points us toward a Mystery and Wonder whose grace we have met in Jesus of Nazareth. Thus we have hope. We know we belong to this side of time, with all its anxieties and insecurities. But from Christ's aspect of eternity, we are confident that the Eternal Creator's criterion of the good and wholeness is what will prevail and what is worthy of allegiance."

Thus hope is not embarrassed to offer a consolation that transcends the universal. Hope's consolation has the power to provide dignity and value for every human life, as each individual projects himself or herself into an uncertain future which, from this side of time, can never be wholly fathomed. "Come!" hope says. "Enter into that future with confidence and courage, knowing that you belong to the Eternal and to the household of faith, and not just to yourself. Know that your life is more than a 'moment of annihilation's waste.'[7] For your Creator loves you and will provide you with a strength that no person, calamity, or disaster can ever take from you."

Love. Finally, there is love. Love both compels the Christian to take the ethical and the universal seriously and allows the believer to be human in a way that transcends the universal and can draw one's neighbor beyond it toward the Eternal. As impor-

---

7. Omar Khayyam's, "The Rubaiyat":

One moment of Annihilation's Waste,
One moment of the Well of Life to Taste.

tant as it is for the Christian to embrace the universal in the interests of justice, it is of course never enough as Christians to embrace the universal alone, since we pursue a higher happiness.

Justice is essential as an ingredient in the achievement of any particular form of universal good; but of equal importance to the Christian is the need to inform (or "invest") one's just acts with love and for the most direct and simple of reasons. For such is the way God loves and such is the motivating Spirit behind God's own acts. For "God is love" (1 John 4:8) and is compassionate (Exod. 22:27). Hence, to her commitment to the universal, the Christian brings love. In doing so, she loves as she has been loved and bears witness to the power of love as life's highest value. In doing so, she becomes part of God's transforming work in the world and fulfills Paul's words: "Do not be conformed to this world but be transformed by the renewal of your mind, that you may prove what is the will of God, what is good and acceptable and perfect" (Rom. 12:2).

The Role of the Virtues in a Pluralistic Age

Is it possible for the virtues, or even a theory of virtue, to contribute toward the best-ordering of society in a pluralistic age? The answer, of course, is "Yes."

There are no pure theocracies anywhere on the globe today, though Tibet once was and a resurgent Islam has sought to reestablish Moslem jurisprudence where it can. Nor are there any pure democracies where the people *(demos)* actually determine their own fate without the mediation of elected representatives. All of which is for the better. Nonetheless, the virtues are significant and have the capacity to unite human beings around a core of mutually respected attitudes and values that, in turn, have the power to shape actions and judgments toward achieving what is good in any culture and under any form of government.

For example, Ross's *prima facie* duties of fidelity, gratitude, justice, beneficence, self-improvement, and nonviolence are essentially "person-enhancement" values that underlie the hopes and sentiments of all peoples. They advance not only an individual's good but the good of all the citizens of the societies which embrace them. To deny this is tantamount to extolling the very vices these virtues oppose: infidelity, ingratitude, injustice, malevolence, and self-indulgence. One needs only to stop and reflect critically about the laws of one's own land. To what extent do they promote justice, self-improvement, and noninjury? Or to what extent do they erode fidelity and gratitude, or promote separation, injury, injustice, or the subjugation of women and children?

As the modern world edges past forms of oppressive government, there is nothing inherent in democracy per se to guarantee the promotion of person-enhancement values. Greed and fear still fuel many economies and dictate foreign policies as well as determine private lifestyles. The feminist analysis of woman's subordination challenges all to venture radical changes in what one thinks, believes, and does regarding women. Furthermore, Ross's duties remind all that there are realities (e.g., the neighbor) and common commitments that transcend the private world of self and thus rightfully function to restrain selfish ambitions.

All six of Ross's duties witness to that ethical and universal dimension that defines human existence as much as self-enhancement does. Such virtues remind society that persons live for more than self or the personal, and that human beings are incomplete apart from each other. Virtues that bind the individual to one's neighbor are as essential as virtues that mold one's personal development and character. Virtues that encourage men and women to venture Eisler's "partnership-modeled" societies are needed everywhere. Such virtues are required for any true person-enhancement or self-realization to occur.

The virtues are doubly significant to a religious person of any religion. On the one hand, the virtues witness to what a believer understands to be that ultimate reality and truth that embraces and underlies the universe — that it and humankind do not exist for themselves alone but belong to God. Thus, the virtues witness to a Wonder and Transcendence that alone best defines and provides for one's highest possibility of personal development and communal fulfillment. On the other hand, the universal virtues unite the religious person at an ethical and spiritual level that has the power to meld persons together into more humane and just social units. As such, the virtues point to the Eternal Law and Divine Will for all human beings and their best possible "well-ordering." Rather than viewing each other with suspicion, the fact that religious groups share numerous values in common ought to act more as an incentive for uniting persons behind just and humane legislation and global concerns than as a cause for suspicion and division.

The Second Vatican Council set an important precedent when it recognized the moral and spiritual validity of non-Christian religions, particularly at the universal level. In so doing, it underscored humanity as a fellow-humanity, created for ends that far exceed a life based on self, self-gain, greed, fear, spite, or vengeance. Christians in particular ought to welcome this affirmation of common humanity, since it validates beingness as something intended for reciprocity with a Wonder and Transcendence far greater than oneself and for loving reciprocity with others. This is especially true in an age of immense greed and self-indulgence, with a crumbling commitment to social values, the loss of a true sense of self-identity, an age of widescale homelessness, misery, and destitution, religious separatism, and of ethnic prejudice, rejection, and divisiveness that is coupled with anger, economic impoverishment, and low self-esteem. The virtues remind our era that our common humanity outweighs these vices. Indeed, our common values have the power to help us regain that loss of vision that promotes and cherishes human good. Commitment to the virtues advance one's sense of self and, therefore, one's experience of the good; and it advances one's neighbor's good, thereby, in the Christian faith, promoting God's desired will for all.

With Christian charity, Vatican II declares:

> [The church] gives primary consideration . . . to what human beings have in common and to what promotes fellowship among them.
>
> For all peoples comprise a singe community, and have a single origin, since God made the whole race of men dwell over the entire face of the earth. . . . One also is their final goal: God

(Declaration on the Relationship of the Church to Non-Christian Religions).[8]

The document goes on to praise Hinduism, Buddhism, and Islam as religions which guard a high esteem for the moral life and promote appropriate paths that lead to its attainment. Thus it urges all Christians to "acknowledge, preserve, and promote the spiritual and moral goods found among these men, as well as the values in their society and culture."[9]

An understanding of the instrumental value of the virtues can unite religious persons of good will worldwide to champion together the things that make for good. Religious persons do not have to bow to the godless forces of self, the subjugation of man or woman, sex, hate, indifference, materialism, and national interest when determining what advances humankind's highest good. With Peter, they have an obligation to work within the social and political institutions that affect common humanity. With Hinduism, they can honor its devotion to *dharma,* to *ahimsa* (nonviolence), to customs, values, and commitments that enhance the family and deepen the true self. With Buddhism, they can respect the historical Buddha's *Dhamapada* and his emphasis on selflessness, truthfulness, gratitude, alertness, self-discipline, and simplicity. With Islam, one can esteem the *Quran* and Mohammed's love for a life surrendered to Allah, in which God's merciful will for believers takes precedence over the greed and selfishness which Moslems see predominating in the West. Finally, with Confucius and Mencius, one can affirm the values of benevolence *(jen),* moral wisdom *(chih),* and propriety *(li).* And in the struggle with greed and self that ensues believers can agree with the Dalai Lama that the practice of "kindness" is essential in any confrontation with the world and its values. Indeed, for both Jews and Christians, that very "kindness" is an echo of God's compassion and *hesed* love, by means of which God comes to humanity in both the Hebrew Bible and the New Testament and nudges the hearts of humankind worldwide.

8. *The Documents of Vatican II,* ed. Walter M. Abbott, S.J. (New York: Corpus Books, 1966), 660-61.
    9. Ibid., 663.

At the same time, while honoring each other's particularity, religious persons ought to deplore readily the new resurgence toward separatism, nationalism, exclusivism, genderism, and ethnicity which we see resurfacing around the globe. Anything that separates sisters and brothers from their neighbor's good must be challenged in the name of the Creator-God, who loves and claims us all. Anything that exalts one neighbor at the expense of the other must be resisted by the tribunal of common concern as failing to enhance mutual worldwide need and support of one another.

Conclusion

In his own quest for a criterion that can transcend good and evil, Nietzsche singles out three "Images of Man," as he calls them, which, in his estimation, still possess power to "urge mortal men to transfigure their own lives."[10] They are the "images" inspired by Rousseau, Goethe, and Schopenhauer.

In Nietzsche's analysis, Rousseau's image encourages a return to nature and extols the virtues of nature as a cleansing agent, able to purge away all modern vices. Indeed, this temptation exists within the feminist movement itself. But Nietzsche rejects Rousseau's principle of nature on the grounds that a career spent in harmonizing itself with nature is beneath the highest human purpose. Indeed, the Bible's own quarrel with baalism and Goddess symbolism asserts the same.

Goethe's greatest achievement, Nietzsche proposes, is his Faust. According to Nietzsche, Goethe's Faust symbolizes an insatiable hunger to experience and to observe as much of life as possible. But in the process, Nietzsche charges, Faust wastes himself in ancillary pursuits, becoming a spectator, a traveler, an observer of life, who ultimately degenerates into a Philistine.

In the final analysis, it is only Schopenhauer, claims Nietzsche, who provides men and women with the best "Image of Man" with

10. Nietzsche, *All Too Human,* cited by Clive, *The Philosophy of Nietzsche,* 348.

his conviction that humankind's highest end is "to tell the truth."
It is, says Neitzsche, the task of taking upon oneself "the pain of
telling the truth."[11]

However excellent this last image is, the biblical story confronts God's people with one that is supremely suited to human
beings and genuinely points to that truth that transcends mortality.
It is the fact that "God created humankind in his image; . . . male
and female he created them" (NRSV Gen. 1:27), and in so doing
bestowed upon each sex incredible potential for intellectual growth
and moral development, that each may find life's highest joy in
reciprocity and fellowship with God and with one another.

In century after century, Christianity's true saints have committed themselves to the pain of telling this truth. For they know
of no higher truth that can lift humankind above the foibles of
self and complete one's wholeness as a human being. Thus, in
humble surrender to God, whose grace in Jesus Christ cleanses
and empowers believers, God's true saints praise a life of virtue,
devoted to *love of God* and *love of neighbor* and, casting themselves on God, attempt to actualize this love with all their heart
and soul.

11. Ibid., 350.

Selected Bibliography

Aquinas, Thomas. *Treatise on the Virtues*. Trans. John A. Oesterle. Englewood Cliffs, N.J.: Prentice-Hall, 1966.

Aristotle. *Nicomachean Ethics*. Translated by Martin Oswald. The Library of Liberal Arts. New York: Macmillan Publishing Company, 1962.

Barnette, Henlee H. *Introducing Christian Ethics*. Nashville: Broadman Press, 1961.

Bloesch, Donald G. *Freedom For Obedience: Evangelical Ethics in Contemporary Times*. San Francisco: Harper & Row, Publishers, 1987.

Casey, John. *Pagan Virtue: An Essay in Ethics*. Oxford: Clarendon Press, 1990.

Christ, Carol P. & Judith Plaskow. *Womanspirit Rising: A Feminist Reader in Religion*. San Francisco: HarperSanFrancisco, 1979.

Crossin, John W. *What Are They Saying About Virtue*. New York: Paulist Press, 1985.

Dent, N. J. H. *The Moral Psychology of the Virtues*. Cambridge: Cambridge University Press, 1984.

Eisler, Riane. *The Chalice & The Blade: Our History, Our Future*. San Francisco: HarperSanFrancisco, 1988.

Foot, Philippa. *Virtues and Vices and Other Essays in Moral Philosophy*. Berkeley and Los Angeles: University of California Press, 1978.

179

Geach, Peter Thomas. *The Virtues.* Cambridge: Cambridge University Press, 1977.

George, Augustine, et al. *Gospel Poverty: Essays in Biblical Theology.* Translated by M. D. Guinan. Chicago: Franciscan Herald Press, 1977.

Guardini, Romano. *The Virtues: On Forms of Moral Life.* Translated by Stella Lange. Chicago: H. Regnery Co, 1967.

Haring, Bernard. *The Law of Christ.* 2 Vols. Translated by Edwin G. Kaiser. Westminster, Maryland: The Newman Press, 1963.

Harned, David Baily. *Faith and Virtue.* Philadelphia: United Church Press, 1973.

Hauerwas, Stanley. *Character and the Christian Life: A Study in Theological Ethics.* San Antonio: Trinty University Press, 1975.

————. *Vision and Virtue.* Notre Dame: Fides/Claretian, 1974.

MacIntyre, Alasdair C. *After Virtue: A Study in Moral Theory.* Notre Dame: University of Notre Dame Press, 1984.

Maston, T. B. *Biblical Ethics: A Guide to the Ethical Message of the Scriptures from Genesis through Revelation.* Mercer University Press, 1982.

Meilaender, Gilbert. *The Theory and Practice of Virtue.* South Bend, Indiana: University of Notre Dame Press, 1984.

Mott, Stephen Charles. *Biblical Ethics and Social Change.* New York: Oxford University Press, 1982.

Neill, Stephen Charles. *The Christian Character.* New York: Association Press, 1955.

Nietzsche, Friedrich W. *"On the Genealogy of Morals" and "Ecce Homo."* Translated by Walter Kaufmann. New York: Vintage Books, 1989.

Olsson, Karl A. *Seven Sins and Seven Virtues.* New York: Harper, 1962.

Pieper, Josef. *The Four Cardinal Virtues: Prudence, Justice, Fortitude, Temperance.* Translated by Richard and Clara Winston et al. New York: Harcourt, Brace & World, 1965.

Porter, Jean. *The Recovery of Virtue.* Louisville: Westminster/John Knox Press, 1990.

Ross, William David. *The Right and the Good.* Oxford: Clarendon Press, 1930.

Wallace, James D. *Virtues & Vices.* Ithaca, New York: Cornell University Press, 1978.

White, R. E. O. *Biblical Ethics.* Atlanta: John Knox Press, 1979.

Yearly, Lee H. *Mencius and Aquinas: Theories of Virtue and Conceptions of Courage.* New York: State University of New York Press, 1990.